#We *Are* Rent

Free Riding

The idea of the self-devouring process originated in ancient Egypt. The symbol was a circular snake or a dragon (called *ouroboros*) which ate its tail. Classical Greece reversed the meaning, and interpreted the symbol as renewal of life, representing wholeness or infinity. Today, we might reinterpret the image as the symbol of free riding, whose cannibalistic culture devours the human capacities on which it depends for its own existence.

#We*Are*Rent

Book 2

Rent Seeking:
the Crime against Humanity

FRED HARRISON

Land
Research
Trust

First published in 2022 by
Land Research Trust
7 Kings Road
Teddington
TW11 OQB, UK

Land
Research
Trust

landresearchtrust.org

British Library Cataloguing in Publication Data
A CIP catalogue record of this book is available
from the British Library

ISBN 978-0-9956351-7-3

Design by Ian Kirkwood
ikdesign.scot

Printed by IngramSpark

"What has destroyed every previous civilisation has been the tendency to the unequal distribution of wealth and power. This same tendency, operating with increasing force, is observable in our civilisation today, showing itself in every progressive community, and with greater intensity the more progressive the community. Wages and interest tend constantly to fall, rent to rise, the rich to become very much richer, the poor to become more helpless and hopeless, and the middle class to be swept away."

Henry George,
Progress and Poverty, Bk 10, Ch. 4.

#We*Are*Rent

Book 2

Rent Seeking:
the Crime against Humanity

Contents

2028
Time Up

For the first time in history, one generation holds the fate of our species in its hands. Mine: the baby boomers, born when soldiers returned home from World War II. Over our lifetime, we have become aware of the threats to the survival of our species. We can meet that challenge by creating an authentic democracy.

It has been a long journey. Ten thousand years ago, humans shifted from tribal communities to urban settlements. For leadership, they trusted their holy men: the priests. Then, they progressed to secular leaders: the princes. Finally, with the emergence of modern civilisation, authority was located in monarchs. Courtiers in the temples and palaces, however, undermined the process of social evolution. From their positions in the inner counsels, they spotted ways to enrich themselves by abusing the resources that sustained their civilisations. They betrayed the trust of the people.

Archaeologists identified the turning points by excavating the sands of time.

▶ **Mesopotamia 2000 BC:** Sumerian priests and princes had guided people to prosperity. Then usury secured a toehold. Families lost their land, communities ruptured and the once flourishing city-states of antiquity were terminated.

▶ **Greece 800 BC:** indebtedness shredded people's lives. They revolted as oligarchs assembled land into large estates. In its weakened political state, Greece was absorbed into the colonising culture of the Roman Empire.

▶ **Rome 200 AD:** centuries of development ended as farmers lost land to oligarchs. Bread and circuses deployed to mollify the landless. Caesars embarked on imperial expansion, but they capitulated to the barbarians.

The beauty of the intellectual and aesthetic achievements of those civilisations distract us from the ugly reality. Some individuals flouted what had become the universal values which made possible the emergence of early humans out of nature. They incubated a culture of cheating, which enabled them to live by riding on other people's backs. In doing so, they rendered their civilisations unsustainable. Communities collapsed as the free riders devoured the resources needed to renew the infrastructure of humanity.

Scholars who investigate the existential threats of the 21st century do not share my thesis. They attribute the threats to *complexity*. Urban society is "a non-equilibrium thermodynamic or dissipative system that must maintain a minimum level of available exergy to avoid entropic decay and a yet higher level to permit physical growth". Inability to sustain themselves is attributed to "the ongoing expansion of human endeavours" which "will continue to result in the Earth System's limits being exceeded and the system being moved out of equilibrium".[1]

Scientists, who have now issued a "code red" warning on the threats from climate warming, do not share my interpretation of humanity as a self-sustaining species. Their general assumption is that we are exclusively dependent on nature for the energy that we need to consume. The existential threat, therefore, is a matter of simple arithmetic. If there are too many people relative to the energy supplied by nature, something has to give. Ergo, collapse of civilisation. This doctrine places primary emphasis on Gaia, rather than the Social Galaxy, and diminishes the role of human agency. We are distracted from the malign role of "bad actors" whose culture of cheating causes the collapse of civilisations by stealing the resources that are required to sustain human activity.

This misdiagnosis stems from a superficial understanding of how humans steered themselves out of nature. Early humans did not evolve by merely "adapting" to nature. As explained in Chapter 1 of Book 1, our primitive ancestors evolved a dynamic process that enabled them to create and channel a unique flow of energy. This meant that, to form themselves into a distinctive species, they had to supplement the laws of nature with laws that regulated their behaviour. They created a Social Galaxy, a self-regulating space that was linked to, but not exclusively dependent on, the laws that govern the universe. To turn themselves into *Homo sapiens*, they had to produce and pool a unique flow of energy. The technical term for those resources is economic rent. I abbreviate that concept as Rent, to distinguish it from commercial rent. Rent is the net flow of resources over and above what people need for their personal subsistence. By decoding its significance, we come to understand the full horror of the catastrophes that now challenge humanity.

1. N. King and A. Jones (2021), "An Analysis of the Potential for the Formation of 'Nodes of Persisting Complexity', *Sustainability* (13), p.2.

Box I.1 **What drives humanity?**

Scholars are trying to determine whether culture or genetics is the major driving force in the evolution of Homo sapiens. On balance, culture is favoured because of its facility for transmitting information faster than biological evolution.* The value of research projects, however, is compromised by the failure to take into account the binary nature of the human personality. Co-existing within each person is the private life, and the social life. The social side of life evolved because of the willingness of individuals to generate the net resources that could be invested in the sociogenic assets that define human beings.

The role of language was vital in the evolutionary project, which is why the words used to communicate knowledge are of significance.† We are obliged to be vigilant in protecting the integrity of the words that we use. I will explain why, for the benefit of the free riders, it was necessary to mangle the concept of Rent. Mind-bending was a major strategy for privatising society's net income.

* Timothy M. Waring *et al* (2017), The Coevolution of economic institutions and sustainable consumption via cultural group selection", *Ecological Economics*, 131(January); Timothy M. Waring and Zachary T. Wood (2021), Long-term gene–culture coevolution and the human evolutionary transition, *Proceedings of the Royal Society B: Biological Sciences*.

† Helen Taylor *et al* (2021), The Evolution of Complementary Cognition, *Cambridge Archaeological Journal*.

Rent is the one analytical concept that is missing from scientific investigations into the origins of our species. The implications are mortal. We cannot plan for the further evolution of humanity while the terms on which we have arrived at the current crisis are garbled (Box I.1). Solving the existential crises is contingent on a clear understanding of the concept of Rent.

To achieve the overview of those crises, and how they are interlinked, we must begin by acknowledging the creative relationship between nature, early humans and their communities. This trilogy enabled our earliest ancestors to create the net flow of resources (energy), which they pooled for the common good. They developed customs to inhibit behaviour that deviated from the practise of sharing those resources. Rent is the essence of the triadic relationship. Breach that relationship, and tragedy follows.

Figure I.1 **Symptoms of privatised Rent**

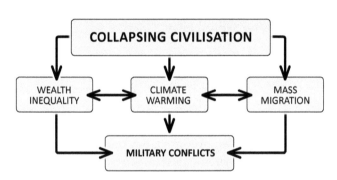

By haemorrhaging Rent into private pockets, the energy needed to create or renew the inter-generational legacy assets ebbs away. Sustain that process of rent seeking for long enough, and the social edifice starts to collapse. Fig. I.1 schematically illustrates some of the symptoms.

The existential crisis needs to be analysed under four primary headings.

Society

Rent privatisation triggers income and wealth gaps. Governments resort to taxing the earned incomes of the working population. A savage discrimination is injected into public policy. One result is the loss of people's right to remain in the communities of their birth. When the commons are enclosed, they are displaced. When homes become unaffordable, they are priced out.

Ecology

Damage was inflicted on the environment from the outset of industrialisation. To maximise the Rent of coal – to enrich the landlords who owned the coal seams beneath their estates - governments did not levy heavenly Rents on those who emitted carbon waste from their combustion engines. Had they done so, engineers would have invented clean technologies to power the railway locomotives and the factory machines.

Demography

Land grabs and economic crises forced people to migrate to North America or Australia in search of a better life. Though colonialism, indigenous communities were displaced from their traditional territories. People were impoverished, but the rent seekers got rich by exploiting the resources of nature.

Military

Through the maldistribution of incomes, people and resources, stresses provoke periodical eruptions of organised violence. This takes the form of individual criminality, civil conflicts and wars between territorial neighbours. Organised gangs and political autocrats exploit these dislocations to appropriate the population's net income.

These four elements interact with each other to intensify the crises. The common feature is the erosion of the energy that people need to pool to sustain their humanity. Free riding – a culture of cheating –

► *disrupts* personal welfare: mind and body, as people lose the capacity to maintain personal welfare because of the barriers to earning a living created by taxation;

► *disrupts* relations between people: subordinating that section of the population that is forced to work for wages which (after taxation) are insufficient for their needs;

► *disrupts* the Social Galaxy's relationship with the universe: degradation of top soils, destruction of forests and waste dumped into the rivers, oceans and the heavens.

All of this to accommodate the culture of cheating!

The dislocated social structure

We could have avoided the existential crises, which now threaten civilisation. As early as the 1820s, a cost/benefit analysis (CBA) would have revealed the existential risks from coal-fired combustion engines. Remedial action was needed as the effects of greenhouse gas revealed themselves in the 1860s. The commercial production of motor vehicles with internal combustion engines did not begin until 1886. Three decades in which to react to the prospects of climate warming and apply the precautionary principle!

Cynics will argue that, at the dawn of industrialisation, the scientific method and the knowledge base were not capable of delivering a comprehensive impact assessment, even if the political will existed to permit such an appraisal. That excuse does not exist today. Yet, researchers still fail to provide the comprehensive CBAs that would reveal the full horror of the existential challenges that face humanity. We need not share the fate of the ancient Egyptians or the citizens of Babylon.

We must establish root causes, the order of priorities for remedial action, and relink rights with responsibilities. A granular account that personalises the threats will enable readers to assess the risks for themselves.

Two viruses

The year 2020 was the story of two viruses and the need to find solutions.

Out of nature came Covid-19. Millions more would have died if scientists in their laboratories had failed to find the antidote. In record time, they delivered the vaccine.

The second virus was social in its origin: the symptoms manifested themselves in a variety of forms, including unequal outcomes in people's life chances. Lawmakers, however, instead of applying the social vaccine, made things worse.

To sustain their populations during the pandemic, western governments had no choice but to pour huge sums of money into the global economy. The negative consequences, however, could have been neutralised if governments had simultaneously reframed their fiscal policies. In doing so, they would have begun to treat all citizens as equals. They did not do so, which is why the post-pandemic economic challenges need to be analysed under four headings.

1. Sovereign debts at stratospheric heights.
2. Cost of borrowing money near or below zero.
3. Extensive bankruptcies of enterprises.
4. Explosive growth in house prices.

National treasuries, and central banks, have to negotiate their way through the debt-laden financial minefield. Given the tools authorised by lawmakers, they cannot do so without creating further dislocations to the economy (curbing the growth of jobs) and society (accelerating the widening gap in the distribution of wealth).

The OECD (Organisation for Economic Cooperation and Development) provided the data on wealth inequality. In the run-up to the pandemic, 40% of households held only 3% of total private net wealth. The wealthiest 10% of households held 52% of the wealth "pie". The maldistribution was at its starkest in the US, where the top 10% owned close to 80% of total wealth. This meant that, going into the pandemic, households in the bottom half of the wealth distribution were most vulnerable to loss of jobs and income. They had to borrow more, sell more of their remaining assets, and end up deeper in debt than the wealthiest households.[2]

Real estate played the single most significant role in the story of wealth maldistribution. It accounted for 61% of gross assets for the bottom 40% of households. The share was only 34% for the top 10%, but this statistic bears closer examination. The OECD claimed that stock prices outpaced house prices during the 2010-2020 decade (the recovery phase of the 18-year business cycle: see Prologue). This is misleading. Yields from stocks and shares include Rent revenue extracted by enterprises either directly (from the ownership of real estate), or indirectly (with natural resources traded by their businesses). Rent overshadows the other streams of revenue. This is why, coming out of the pandemic, governments and central bankers found themselves trapped in a fiscal inferno (Fig. I.2). The unequal outcomes from historically low interest rates created political dilemmas and deepened the economic crisis.

- ► Low or zero interest rates enabled governments to fund sovereign debts and encourage private capital formation. Cheap mortgages, however, encouraged wealthy people to pour money into the housing market.

- ► Skyrocketing property prices prevented young people and low-income families from accessing homes at affordable prices. This reduced labour mobility, constrained productivity and aroused political discontent.

---

2. OECD (2021), "Inequalities in Household Wealth and Financial Insecurity of Households", Policy Brief.

► Tax policies privileged wealthy investors. By purchasing real estate, they diminished (even eliminated) their fiscal liabilities. This reduced government revenue, cut funds for public services and widened the wealth gap.

Figure I.2 **The Fiscal Inferno**

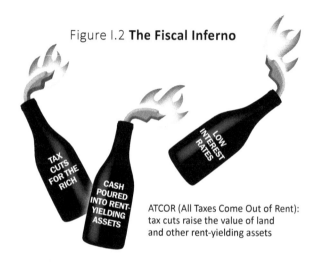

ATCOR (All Taxes Come Out of Rent):
tax cuts raise the value of land
and other rent-yielding assets

Central bankers faced morally challenging choices. By raising interest rates, they would deter capital formation and job creation. But low interest rates privileged the wealthiest asset owners, who would grow even wealthier from the accelerating increases in the value of residential property. Jay Powell, chair of the US Federal Reserve, acknowledged that prospect. "Does anyone seriously argue that we should try to stop that from happening by raising rates at the cost of [not] putting people at the bottom end of the income spectrum back to work? No. Of course we wouldn't do that".[3]

---

3. Joe Rennison (2021), "Fed's fine intentions in fighting the pandemic fuel record levels of inequality", *Financial Times*, July 26.

Keeping interest rates low helps to drive up house prices. Higher interest rates would dampen house prices, but curb capital formation and the creation of jobs.

By choosing to retain low interest rates, governments acting in the name of the people authorise the growing gap between rich and poor. They reinforce the decline in social resilience; expand the despair among those at the bottom of the income scales; and heighten the tensions between people of different race and creed. Cumulatively, this deepens the public distrust of politicians while marooning future generations on mountains of ever-expanding debts.

The richest households celebrate! The value of their Rent-yielding assets grows as they further reduce the tax paid into the public purse. Meanwhile, politicians remain hostages to the doctrines that favour those who ride free on the backs of the working population.

The organising mechanism at the heart of this trap is the tax-and-tenure nexus. It operates because of ATCOR (all taxes come out of Rent). No matter how tortuous the route taken by taxes, they ultimately fall on Rent. That is why the free riders lobby governments to reduce taxes. A cut in the rate of income tax triggers a rise in the value of Rent-yielding assets. Adam Smith spelt out this ATCOR effect in detail. His illustrations are summarised in the Appendix.

The inevitable outcome from the fiscal inferno is the acceleration of society towards the precipice.

Civilisations have been here before. There is a comprehensive solution. It is a "silver bullet" policy, which The Experts claim does not exist. The policy was available to resolve problems in the past, but it was rejected. Its absence from the toolboxes of national treasuries today, therefore, is intentional.

Building back better

If, in history, lawmakers had acted to rescue their societies from the crises they faced – by "building back better" – our Social Galaxy would not be hanging on a thin thread. Those missed opportunities offer insights into our future. We can review them to stimulate our resolve to avoid similar mistakes in the future. This entails exercises in counterfactual history.

► In 1705, Scottish economist John Law proposed that national currencies should be anchored in the value of land. If his advice had been followed in Scotland and then in England, the 1707 treaty signed by the two nations would have located the United Kingdom on a unique footing.

Both countries adopted land taxes in the 16th century. Integrating that fiscal policy with the monetary system would have caused the economy of the British Isles to flourish on a sustainable basis: no busts after finance-fuelled booms. The insatiable appetite of rent seeking would have been suppressed, governance would have been directed by responsible fiscal policy, thereby avoiding sovereign debt. As a result, there would have been no need for Britain to impose the taxes on its American colonists which provoked a war.

► In 1774, Louis XVI appointed Anne Robert Jacques Turgot (1727–1781) as his First Minister of State. Turgot had witnessed how trade and tax policies undermined the welfare of the peasants. He detected revolution in the air. His antidote was a tax on land values. Louis declined. Turgot was sacked.

Turgot was a member of the Physiocratic school of philosophy that wanted to chart a new economic course for France. Had he succeeded, there would have been no need for a violent

Revolution, a constitutional monarchy might have evolved and Napoleon would not have become emperor on the back of his continent-wide war. The course of European history would have been dramatically different from the one that emerged as military conflicts leading to two world wars.

▶ In 1776, Adam Smith studied the Physiocratic doctrines and wrote *The Wealth of Nations*. His political economy was designed to optimise the freedom of citizens and elevate the quality of governance. Central to that project was the fiscal system. Raising revenue from ground rent was a "peculiarly suitable" way to fund the public sector and emancipate people who worked for their living.

One of Smith's admirers was Prime Minister Pitt the Younger. If he had followed Smith's advice, he would have upgraded the land tax to harmonise the interface between the public and private sectors – between citizens and the state. The Industrial Revolution would have coursed through the nation to deliver inclusive prosperity. Instead, he innovated the Income Tax in 1798. One effect was to encourage the Captains of Industry to channel profits into the purchase or construction of country estates, to ape the lifestyles of the aristocracy.

▶ In 1797, Thomas Paine published *Agrarian Justice*. He explained why every holder of land "owes to the community a ground-rent (for I know of no better term to express the idea) for the land which he holds; and it is from this ground-rent that the fund proposed in this plan is to issue". Paine engaged with republicans in America and France, as well as lawmakers in Britain, to promote his agenda.

Paine sketched the terms of a Welfare State. Ground rent would be sufficient to finance government while funding the education of children of low-income families; provide security for the disabled and aged; and, among other services, would cover the cost of funerals of the poor. Paine's plan was not adopted. Children would not have been sent up the chimneys of "dark satanic mills" in the 19th century if governments had taken his analysis to heart.

▶ In 1879, American journalist Henry George took up the cause of tax reform in *Progress and Poverty*. That text laid the foundations for the first global reform movement. In Britain, the Liberal Party championed the cause and almost succeeded in creating a humane form of governance. Its budget of 1910 initiated the collection of Rent to fund unemployment and care of the aged.

Landlords in the House of Lords would have none of it, but they were prevented from blocking the legislation in 1910. Revenge came 10 years later, when they engineered the cancellation of the land tax. Rent that had been collected was paid back to the landlords. The UK launched into the Roaring '20s and crashed into the Depression of the '30s.

This catalogue of what-might-have-been dreams alerts us to the profound challenge facing reformers today. To alter the course of history, lawmakers need the democratic consent of the majority who own real estate. In the UK, the politically most influential voting group is comprised of my generation of homeowners: the post-war generation which benefited from the Welfare State and who own high value properties. Can we fulfil our humanitarian responsibilities? Or will we cling to the capital gains from the land beneath our homes while watching the collapse of civilisation?

The decisive decade

That is how President Joe Biden characterised the 2020s: the decisive decade.

Biden is a sincere politician, but his status – the most powerful politician in the world – does not immunise him from the delusions that are sealing the fate of western democracies. His project for reforming the United States will fail. If the rest of us continue to share his delusions, the price paid by humanity will be terrible.

To appreciate the nature of the challenges that we all now face, recall how, as Barak Obama's Vice-President, Biden sought to stem the flow of migrants from the Latin South. He failed. Now he has passed that poisoned chalice to *his* Vice-President, Kamala Harris. The goal: stem the flow of hungry children up to the US border. *She* will fail. Not for the want of trying. The problem is that these powerful politicians are puppets manipulated by a culture that denies people the right to remain in their home communities.

At immediate stake is western democracy.

I will address the global dimensions of the crisis in Book 3. Here, I will highlight the crisis in the Anglosphere to test the proposition that the fiscal remedy remains the central strategy for solving socially significant problems. The USA and the UK, in particular, will be spotlighted; the USA because it considers itself to be the birthplace of modern democracy, the UK because of its pivotal role in fostering the existential threat to humanity across the globe.

Enter Caesar

The termination of civilisation is a drawn-out process. Oswald Spengler (1880-1936), the German polymath who authored *The Decline of the West*, gave that process a name: *Caesarism*. In Europe, this phase originated with Napoleon as a "kind of government which, irrespective of any constitutional formulation that it may have, is in its inward self a return to thorough form-lessness". Formless in appearance, perhaps, but with an internal mechanism that gave it direction. Spengler explained how parliamentary politics fed the interests that would dominate the dying phase of European civilisation.

Philosophers of the Enlightenment defined democracy as government "by and for the people". Spengler was not deluded. From 1832, he noted,

> the English nobility itself, through a series of prudent measures, drew the bourgeoisie into *co-operation* with it, but under its continued guidance and, above all, in the framework of tradition, within which consequently the young talent grew up.[4]

The nobility co-opted the "young talent" into their values and institutions. Scholars call that process *socialisation*. The abrasive description is *brainwashing*.[5] In terms of the embedded system of values, nothing changed within the framework of parliamentary politics. Spengler continued:

> Democracy thus actualized itself here so that the Government remained strictly 'in form' – the old aristocratic form – while the individual was free to practise politics according to his bent.

Parliamentary politics evolved in the 18th century by employing techniques that included the purchase of votes to ensure compliance with the wishes of the landed class.[6] The franchise was an illusion. It did not signify the right to *self*-determination. With brutal frankness, Spengler noted

> The more nearly universal a franchise is, the *less* becomes the power of the electorate.

4. Oswald Spengler (1932), *The Decline of the West*, London: George Allen & Unwin, Vol 2, p.412, n.2. Emphasis in original.
5. The Chinese Communist Party provides a real time public display of brainwashing–aka acculturation – on a massive scale, re-shaping the minds and behaviour of its population to fit its ideological purposes.
6. Under Henry Pelham (Prime Minister, 1743-1754), members of the House of Commons were paid £500 or more at the end of each term, depending on the value of the services rendered to the Government.

In engineering the transition from monarchical absolutism to constitutional monarchy, the feudal nobility focused on a single outcome: the preservation of its right to transfer to themselves the nation's Rent. Parliamentary politics were designed to facilitate their financial scam. With utmost subtlety the nobility, aided and abetted by the gentry, hoodwinked people into thinking that power resided with those who voted for representatives who enacted the laws of the land. The scam worked, and it continues to operate in the 21st century.[7]

As a direct result of evolving their culture into one of systematic cheating, an avaricious English aristocracy went in search of an empire. It was successful to the point where, as documented by Spengler, England built the power that enabled it to shape Europe's destiny from Napoleon through to World War 1.

The last 100 years is the story of the embedding of Rent privatisation deeper into Europe. Then – through decolonisation – that culture was embedded in constitutions across the globe. The outcome is paralysis of the political imagination, as reflected in the failures of governance. Reversing this dismal trend depends entirely on how we revisualise the role of Rent in society.

Saving civilisation

I am optimistic. Our globalised civilisation does face extinction, but we can forestall the worst outcomes. We achieve this by empowering people to build defences against the turbulence that marks the end of the epoch of free riding.

---

7. In the UK, the House of Lords is the vanguard that protects the Rent-privatising culture of the nobility. After some reforms, 85 dukes, earls and barons remain in the chamber by the rights created by their forefathers. In return for the generous expenses paid for turning up in Westminster, when they do speak "they are 60% more likely to mention business or personal interests" than the life peers. Gabriel Pogrund and Tom Calver (2021), "Revealed: The truth about peers who are born to rule", *Sunday Times*, March 21.

Given the scale of the psychological shifts that are indispensable, it is incumbent on me to describe how the culture of cheating remains vigilant over legislation (Ch. 1), and how it continues to colonise people's lives in the 21st century (Ch. 2). Chapter 3 offers a vision of how a reformed system would evolve in response to the correct financial reforms. Before tampering with current political structures, however, we must have no doubt that existing political systems are beyond repair (Chs. 4-5). Since the deepest ruptures would be located in people's collective consciousness, we need to appreciate the cathartic benefits of Socratic conversations (Ch. 6). Finally, I describe how an authentic form of democracy would equip nations to realign themselves under problem solving constitutions. The four nations of the British Isles provide the case study (Ch. 7).

The unique opportunity bequeathed to our generation is time limited. The countdown to the convergence of all of the existential crises has begun. The Prologue describes the timetable for change if we wish to avoid the horrors that will otherwise erupt at the end of this decade. We *can* expel the cultural virus that feeds off people's bodies and souls, but the conversation needs to begin immediately.

In 2028, the clock stops.

Fred Harrison

London
January, 2022

2027
Cultural Cannibalism

The year of reckoning. Apocalyptic fears aroused by what lurks at the bottom of the vortex. We arrived at the precipice by betraying the evolutionary formula painfully developed over hundreds of thousands of years.

Taxation and the property rights that underwrite modern nations are the No. 1 threat to civilisation. They now also threaten the viability of humanity itself. This is alarmism in its extreme form, but is it based on bias or objective assessment of facts?

Deviation from the evolutionary blueprint results in dysfunctional behaviour that disrupts people's association with each other, and disturbs their relationship with nature. Trauma pervades such societies.[1] To identify the causes of this state of affairs, we need to distinguish a sane society from one that is actively subverting its own existence. I claim that the evolutionary blueprint provides the universal criteria for judging if a society is degenerating into the state of insanity. Erich Fromm (1900 –1980), a German social psychologist and philosopher, would disagree. To speak of a "sane society", he wrote,

> makes sense only if we assume that there can be a society which is not sane, and this assumption, in turn, implies that there are universal

---

1. Fred Harrison (2012), *The Traumatised Society*, London: Shepheard-Walwyn.

criteria for mental health which are valid for the human race as such, and according to which the state of health of each society can be judged.[2]

Fromm worked within the doctrine that claimed that everything was relative. If correct, this would render difficult the determination of what constitutes a "normal" society. The weaknesses in his diagnostic method surface in his analysis of the conditions that scholars associate with capitalism. He absorbed the prejudices that mischaracterise contemporary society.

To identify the correct remedies, we need to understand the source of ill health in all of its forms – mental, physical and social. Mental ill health, for example, is estimated to cost the global economy anything between $2.5tn and $8.5tn each year in lost productivity.[3] The gains from restoring health are enormous, but contingent on applying cures rather than palliatives.

In Book 1 of *#WeAreRent*, I explained that capitalism is a binary system of economics. It is pathologically split between the value-adding function (as people work for their living), and the value-extracting function (rent seeking on the backs of the working population). Economists exclude free riding from their macro-economic models, treating it as an aberration. In reality, it is a systemic feature of – indeed, the most important driving mechanism within - modern economies. Its anti-productive spirit pollutes enterprises that ostensibly exist to produce value. A conspicuous example is that of construction companies. Officially, they build dwellings. Unofficially, some of them are more interested in stockpiling land in their banks. By *not* building on the sites, investors in those companies are rewarded with windfall capital gains (Box P.1).[4]

2.Erich Fromm (1956) *The Sane Society*, London: Routledge & Kegan Paul, 2nd edn., p.12.
3. Harris A. Eyre *et al* (2020), "The Brain Economy", *RSA Journal* (3), p.44.
4. Stock market valuations often fail to reflect the value of freehold land. Financiers known as "vulture capitalists" specialise in buying companies with borrowed money, using the real estate owned by their prey as collateral. Morrison's, the fourth largest

---

Box P.1 **Why dogs don't give a bone**

Erich Fromm fell into the trap of portraying capitalism as a singular system. Hence his claim that classical economists like David Ricardo swallowed the biological thesis called the "struggle for survival".* He attributed the latter formulation to Charles Darwin, who did not, in fact, invent it. Herbert Spencer adapted Darwin's science-based theory of evolution to suit the financial prejudices of the nobility.** Classical economists imagined an economy *sans* rent seeking, which would result from raising the public's revenue from Rent.

Because he lacked an objective standard for measuring the health of society, Fromm argued that people's "character is definitely determined only by the circumstances under which they live". This had the unintended consequence of diverting attention away from the common cause that disfigures societies of contrasting creeds and geographies.

The contrast between Fromm's subjective approach, and my objective evolutionary method, is illustrated by his reference to Adam Smith's observation on dogs and bones. "Nobody ever saw a dog make a fair and deliberate exchange of one bone for another with another dog."*** Dogs do not trade bones. True. They are not value-adding creatures. Humans need to trade. That cooperation generates the net resources (Rent) that fund society. Otherwise, they would just work for their subsistence. Like dogs.

* Erich Fromm (1956), *The Sane Society*, p.74.
** Fred Harrison (2015), *As Evil Does*, London: Geophilos, pp.28-32.
*** Adam Smith (1776), *The Wealth of Nations*, Bk 1, Ch.2.

Psychoanalysis is an insufficient discipline for evaluating the relevant evidence. The science of ecology is similarly insufficient, from the point of view of mobilising the resources needed for an effective remedy to the myriad disruptions inflicted on Earth. Ecologists developed the concept of the Anthropocene to register the impact of human beings. This geological concept

---

UK supermarket chain, became the target for take-over in 2021. It owned the freeholds of nearly 90% of its 500 stores.

describes human influence over the planet's eco-systems, but in doing so it focuses attention on symptoms rather than root causes. The evolutionary blueprint, which obliges us to deploy a multi-disciplinary approach, equips us to isolate the pathological behaviour that afflicts all societies on Earth today. This, in turn, leads us inexorably to the remedies.

Compounding problems

We interrogate the existential challenge to humanity through four categories of activity: society, ecology, demography and technology. Each has become a compound event that is now beyond the point of precautionary treatment. Each one is a runaway phenomenon that feeds off the others. They all track back to a common cause.

Runaway events emerge when the balancing act within the Social Galaxy is disrupted. Balance is achieved when people produce sufficient net income to renew the legacy assets that sustain their living space. To secure systemic stability, people enforced rules of behaviour to outlaw behaviour that would jeopardise the production of the net resources they needed. By this means – deployed through their moral and spiritual sensibilities – they secured harmony within communities, and in relation to nature. A culture of cheating would violate these arrangements by animating insatiable appetites. Greed becomes a systemic problem when people can accumulate resources without having to work for them. That is when the culture becomes cannibalistic, exercising the power that overwhelms the rate at which Rent is produced and directed to its social purposes. Feedback loops intervene to accelerate the rate of collapse, by further exhausting the resources needed to regain control of the social system. The erosion of those capabilities are most visible in the form of political paralysis and military conflicts. The net effect is the steady erosion of the resilience of the system.

Figure P.1 **Cascading Vectors of Privatised Rent**

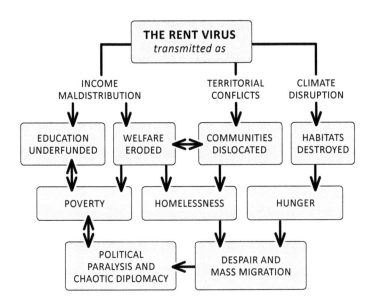

What happens if the four crisis zones – society, ecology, demography and military – combine in a Great Convergence? The rate of depletion of the energy that sustains the Social Galaxy would eclipse the rate at which people produced Rent. Each step in the direction of depletion feeds back on all the parts of the system. Growth of populations exceeds the capacity of governments to fund welfare services. The Big Tech tax dodgers who hoard the spectrum Rents reduce government revenue. Wildfires destroy forests and undermine corporate net-zero emission pledges. The vectors, which transmit the pathologies, erode the resilience of society. Impacts are generational, geographical and geopolitical (Fig P.1).

The cumulative impact is the cultural cannibalism that terminates civilisation. In this volume, however, I am going further. *Human life on planet Earth is now at stake.*

Any one of the four catastrophes, by itself, would not be sufficient to extinguish humanity. One of them, however – the demographic crisis – is capable of accelerating the destruction of western civilisation through unfettered migration. A pincer process is already visible through the transit routes.

▶ *Out of South America:* across the continent, the interaction between dysfunctional social systems and debased ecological systems is driving people northwards. Venezuela's economic collapse caused 5m people to flee their country, creating the space for criminal gangs to take control.[5] Reuters reported that one Colombian coastal town declared a state of emergency when 15,000 migrants arrived, intending to sail across the Caribbean to the US.[6]

Within the US, stress created by the inflow of migrants is compounded by policy failures in relation to (for example) the availability of affordable housing. Even before the pandemic, millions of families were struggling to pay rents and mortgages. For half a century, the federal government has curbed the public housing stock, reduced financial assistance to renters, and weakened government budgets (by deducting the cost of mortgages from taxable income). Cumulatively, these policies translate into higher house prices and lower public spending, which add further twists of desperation within deprived communities and resentment of newcomers.

---

5. Michael Stott (2019), "Exile plays down hopes for Venezuela talks", *Financial Times*, August 11.
6. https://www.reuters.com/world/americas/us-bound-migrants-fill-colombia-town-covid-19-border-closures-lifted-2021-08-11/

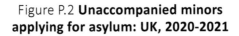

Figure P.2 **Unaccompanied minors applying for asylum: UK, 2020-2021**

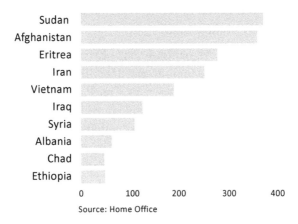

Source: Home Office

▶ *Out of Africa:* Fertility rates exceed the capacity to create employment prospects and produce food, which accelerate the out-migration of desperate people. This is a repetition of what happened to civilisations in antiquity,[7] and to the classical civilisation when the "barbarians" migrated south in the 5th century AD.

Compounding those pressures, autocrats exploit the stresses created by the inflow of migrants into Europe. They seize opportunities to destabilise democratic governments that uphold the rule of law. In Belarus, Alexander Lukashenko drove Iraqi migrants across the European Union's borders as revenge for sanctions imposed on his pariah state.

---

7. Eric H. Cline (2014), *1177 B.C.: The Year Civilisation Collapsed*, Princeton: Princeton University Press.

► *Out of Asia:* Turbulence in the Islamic world has created a permanent flow of refugees into Europe. A recent exodus was on painful display at Kabul airport, when Afghanistan fell to the Taliban. Desperate refugees tried to cling to the hulls of cargo planes rather than remain in the country of their birth.

War-torn Sudan, Afghanistan and Eritrea top the list of nationalities seeking asylum in the UK. The number of lone children seeking refuge is shown in Fig. P.2. That volume will increase towards 2026 and then explode exponentially after the economic crisis that follows the peak in global house prices.

The European Union seeks to repel the migrants by offering cash to create camps in the Middle East. Turkey's Prime Minister, Recep Tayyip Erdogan, would have none of it. He warned the European Union that they would not serve as a "border guard" or as a camp for asylum seekers.[8]

The Great Convergence

By their failure to act decisively, democratic governments are unwittingly conspiring to push their societies over the looming precipice. Nuclear scientists are ringing the alarm bells. They published this prediction on January 27, 2021: "[I]f humanity is to avoid an existential catastrophe – one that would dwarf anything it has yet seen – national leaders must do a far better job of countering disinformation, heeding science, and cooperating to diminish global risks".[9] Their Doomsday Clock was 100 seconds short of midnight – the closest it had ever been in history. We need to locate in its historical context how we arrived at this fateful juncture.

---

8. www.middleeastmonitor.com/20200522-official-says-turkey-is-not-an-eu-border-guard/
9. https://thebulletin.org/2020/01/press-release-it-is-now-100-seconds-to-midnight/

Sixteen hundred years ago, Rome teetered on that precipice. It failed to muster the strength to save itself from collapse. Six hundred years then elapsed before Europe could begin to recover. In the 11th century, the creation of commons in the countryside and guilds in the towns proved to be turning points. The prospects of social renewal ended in the 16th century, however, when the aristocracies of Europe began to dismantle the commons. That history may be summarised in the following statement.

The further a society gravitates away from Rent in its social form, by replacing net income with taxes on wages and earned wealth, the deeper the pathologies that corrode people's welfare and the resilience of their communities.

The privatisation of Rent evolved under the cloak of a culture that actively corrupted behaviour that would otherwise conform to the evolutionary blueprint. That root cause exposes itself as we trace the symptoms through time. The trends shown here are from English history.

▶ **Society in the 17th century**
Destruction of common rights of access to land eroded rural communities. Parliament pretended that this was to raise rural productivity, but it was "essentially a policy directed towards the enhancement of agricultural rents [and] the building up of large and compact landed estates".[10]

Migration to urban slums laid the foundations for the psychological and social stresses that ruptured humane values. Feelings of powerlessness nourished pathological attitudes like animosity towards "others" (those of a different race or creed): minorities blamed for problems that originated in rootlessness. Roots, as Erich Fromm noted, were vital for identity, self-esteem,

---

10. Gilbert Slater (1907), *The English Peasantry and the Enclosure of Common Fields*, London: Archibald Constable, p.vi.

and without them a person "could not bear the isolation and helplessness of this position. He would become insane". Severed from their rights to remain in their home communities, people channelled their frustrations by assuming *faux* identities and creating false enemies.

Power became irresponsible. How else can we characterise the political systems that privilege free riders? Failure to take decisive action on the climate issue, for example, means that governments are planning to abandon whole communities to rising sea levels.[11] Private insurance will not rescue seaside property owners, and governments will lack the resources to relocate their citizens, let alone refugees from abroad.

▶ **Migration in the 18th century**
Deprived of their right to remain in their home communities, millions of Europeans migrated to the Americas and the Antipodes. There, they drove people from their homelands and embedded the economics of rent seeking.

Colonialism transplanted the social neuroses from Europe. Indigenous communities lost their resilience. One outcome was the disruption of traditional constraints on fertility. When combined with the systematic degradation of food-producing topsoil, an irreconcilable imbalance emerged – too many people for the carrying capacity of nature's habitats. According to the Global Footprint Network, people had consumed the stock of ecological resources that the planet was able to regenerate by July 2021 (Fig. P.3).[12] Resources needed to support humans now require the equivalent of 1.7 Earths.

---

11. Tim Wallace (2021), "The boom-and-bust curse of natural disasters", *Daily Telegraph*, August 4.
12. www.footprintnetwork.org/our-work/earth-overshoot-day/

Figure P.3 **Depleting Earth's regenerating powers**

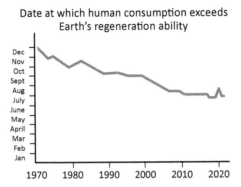

Date at which human consumption exceeds
Earth's regeneration ability

The risks to Europe and North America are incomprehensible. According to one London-based lobby group, the vulnerabilities of 500m Africans qualify them as refugees who might seek admission to rich countries. Their plight was due to "the relentless population explosion and the accompanying poverty and violent tribal rivalry over land and water".[13] The IMF reports that 40 countries endure cycles of low administrative capacity, political instability, conflict and weak economies.[14]

Globally, an estimated one billion children live in countries at "extremely high risk" of climate and environmental shocks. The eco-crises translated into problems of poverty or without adequate housing or sanitation facilities.[15] These add to the pressures to migrate to other continents. The vulnerabilities of poverty-stricken families in host countries compound the needs

13. Sam Akaki (2021), "Safe haven repatriation can solve Africa's migrant crisis", *Financial Times* Letter, Aug. 5.
14. Olusegun Akanbi *et al* (2021), Avoid a Fall or Fly Again: Turning Points of State Fragility, IMF WP/21/133.
15. UNICEF (2021), *The Climate Crisis is a Child Rights Crisis*, New York: United Nations.

of desperate migrants. Across the western world, tens of millions of families are unable to fund the barest minimum living standards and have to rely on food banks.

► **Ecology in the 19th century**
Industrialisation and intensive cultivation of land accelerated the erosion of those parts of nature on which people depended for their sustenance.

With rent seeking entrenched in the centres of power, temperatures began to rise, at first unmonitored. It was not until floods and droughts started to wreak havoc that attention was paid to the climate. But the pricing system was not analysed as out of synch with people's rights and responsibilities. So free riding continued to stride the planet. Governments signed pledges to achieve goals at some future date, pinning their hopes on the removal of carbon with technologies that barely exist.

Political paralysis pervaded governance. The UK government, for example, over a 5-year period, permitted the construction of 570,000 homes that were not resistant to heatwaves. Since 2018, more than 4,000 people died from heat-related issues in England alone. Fatalities mounted in California as lakes dried up and fires consumed huge swathes of forests. The south-west corner of the US faces a potential "mega-drought" – the driest such period in 1,200 years.

Our world is not prepared for an accelerated infusion of plastic in oceans, poison in soils and emission of carbon into the heavens. According to calculations by the International Monetary Fund (IMF), the pandemic will reduce the wealth of nations by $28 trillion in the years to 2025.[16] This reduces government financial capacity to fund existing debts, let alone combat the crises emerging from nature. The cumulative effect will be "cascading

16. https://blogs.imf.org/2020/10/13/a-long-uneven-and-uncertain-ascent/?utm_medium=email&utm_source=govdelivery

crises in the years to come", predicted CNN broadcaster Fareed Zakaria.[17]

► **Technology in the 20th century**
A comprehensive cost/benefit analysis (CBA) would have alerted lawmakers to the threats that might emerge from the digital age. Governments could have controlled the impact of the internet and the onset of robotic power in the workplace.

Charging the full Rent to use the electromagnetic spectrum for on-line commerce would have ensured a smooth phasing in of digital-based services. Corporations like Amazon would not have acquired the power to disrupt High Street retailers. Paying the Rental charge would have encouraged people to discipline their use of "platforms" such as Facebook. Instead, "free" access to smart phone screens nurtured the narcissistic fixations that damaged mental health of children.

Lawmakers, in deeming free communication on the internet a human right, caused the disruptions that emerged in the digital age. Big Tech mutated into new layers of threats to society. Cyber-attacks on infrastructure became the alternative to "hot wars". Autocrats celebrated the low-cost techniques for attacking enemies (Russians actively intervened in elections across Europe and North America). As President Vladimir Putin boasted about Russia's investments in weapons of mass destruction, Britain's military chiefs warned that their army and navy were not fit for purpose. General Lord Dennett, the former Chief of the General Staff, lamented the planned cost-saving reduction of troops in the decade to 2030.[18]

---

17. Fareed Zakaria (2020), *Ten Lessons for a Post-Pandemic World*, London: Allen Lane.
18. Danielle Sheridan (2021), "Former Army chief: English battalions will be hit hardest", *Daily Telegraph*, March 2.

Autocrats have already begun to divert the attention of their people by embarking on military adventures. In Russia's case, Putin is trapped by his dependency on the Rent of gas and petroleum. The looming switch to carbonless cars, and the next economic crisis, will reduce the revenue on which his rogue state relies for its survival. To distract people from home-grown discontent, Russia will intensify the current trend: cyber-attacks on European and US democracies.[19] China has embarked on military displays of intent, with forays in the South China Seas and into Taiwan's air space. To advance its territorial ambitions, China has weaponised the climate emergency. Beijing has warned the US to back away from its theatre of influence, placing cooperation on climate issues at risk. In Africa, Jihadis are replenishing their war chests by taking over the artisanal gold mines in Burkina Faso so that they can fund their Holy Wars.[20]

Trade wars and the technological innovations that cut costs and shift jobs from people to robots will further depress living standards. Globalisation will continue to feature as a scapegoat. The actual driving force behind these trends – the pursuit of Rent wherever it can be found, by whatever means it can be captured – will continue to be ignored.

What hope for humanity?

There are no safe havens left on Earth. Every corner of the planet is riddled with the free riding virus.

To avoid The Great Convergence, we have just five years to design new foundations for a 21st century version of the commons. For if the global economic collapse occurs following the peak in land prices in 2026, the West will become the epicentre of what has been called a "zombie apocalypse". To deploy the organic

---

19. Gen. Sir Nick Carter, Chief of the UK Defence Staff, admits that the risk of a military confrontation with Russia is "the thing that keeps me awake in bed at night". Jack Hardy (2021), "Carter: Russian standoff 'keeping me awake'", *Daily Telegraph*, June 26.
20. Neil Munshi (2021), "Jihadis join the Sahel gold rush", *Financial Times*, June 28.

Figure P.4 **Real land and house price indices 1975 = 100**

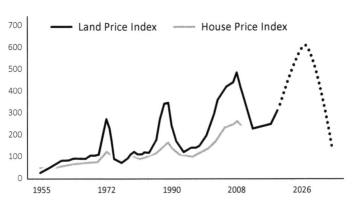

Source: derived from Paul Cheshire (2009), Urban Containment, Housing Affordability and Price Stability – Irreconcilable Goals, London: SERC Policy Paper 4, p.4; extrapolation by the present author.

remedy, however, we need to take account of the timing. Five years are left (at the time of writing) to neutralise the worst of what will come.

The Timetable

Why will house prices peak in 2026?

For the UK, Fig. P.4 illustrates the cyclical trends in the residential property sector since World War 2. House prices are a proxy for the metric that really matters – the Rent (in its capitalised form) that people negotiate to use the locations where they wish live or work.

The UK serves as a key case study for two reasons.

First, the UK dramatises the trends present in the rest of the world. Coming out of the pandemic, global property prices

Figure P.5 **OECD house prices**
Q1 2000 = 100

revealed the presence of "housing fever".[21] Across the OECD group of rich nations, house prices hit the 9.4% mark in mid-2021 – the fastest pace for 30 years.[22] With each cycle, deviations from people's earnings and the cost of living have grown wider (Fig. P.5). In the UK, the contagion across the four member nations was stark, with grievous implications: cyclical booms and busts are treacherous. The last cycle (1992-2010) terminated when the land market peaked in 2007. UK land values declined by over 23%, which far eclipsed the downturn in non-financial assets (-9.6%).[23]

Second, the significance of location values is beyond question. Land constituted 51% of UK net worth in 2016, higher than any other G7 country for which data is available (the average is 39%). The UK is nine percentage points above France (42%), and almost double Germany's 26%.

---

21. Valentina Romei and Chris Giles (2021), "Signs of 'housing fever' surface as global property prices surge", *Financial Times*, August 2
22. OECD (2021), Housing prices. doi: 10.1787/63008438-en (Accessed on August 2, 2021).
23. The UK national balance sheet estimates: 2018, London: Office for National Statistics, Table 1, p.5.

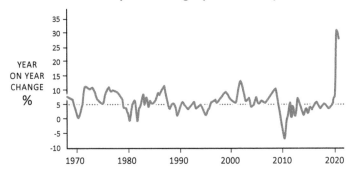

Figure P.6 **US broad money supply: 5% p.a. average (1968-2020)**

Source: Center for Financial Stability (2020), "CFS Monetary Data for the US", Dec. News Release, p.8.

But what determines the 18-year periodicity?

I identified the cause of the cycle in *Power in the Land* (1983). The cycle was present in cultures and geographies as diverse as the UK, USA, Japan and Australia.[24] The land market drove the cycle. In *Boom Bust* (2005), I explained the duration as a function of the long-run average interest rate: 5%. I relied on evidence from the 16th to the 19th centuries to validate my theory that the average cost of mortgages explained the 14-year periods in the property market, which triggered the recessions that J.M. Keynes identified as averaging four years.[25]

The 18-year periodicity was present throughout the 20th century, except for the dislocations caused by world wars. After World War 2, the 5% metric continued to shape investment decisions. The money supply in the US oscillated between 10% and zero, but averaged 5% (Fig. P.6).

---

24. Fred Harrison, *Power in the Land* (2021), 2nd edn., London: Shepheard-Walwyn.
25. Fred Harrison (2005), *Boom Bust: House Prices, Banking and the Depression of 2010*, London: Shepheard-Walwyn.

Figure P.7 **Returns on US housing wealth**

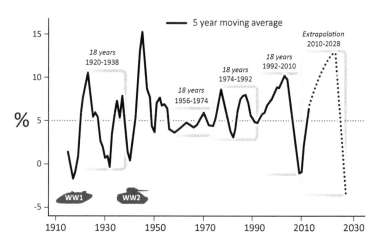

Was the 5% average interest rate operating within the land market? In 2019, researchers who undertook the most exhaustive study to date of housing economics reported that the long-run global yield on housing had averaged around 5% a year. Fig. P.7 illustrates the trends for the USA.[26] The two world wars (along with the Korean War) disturbed the rhythms; but the economy recovered robustly to repeat the 18-year cycles around the expectation of the 5% average return on residential property.

A further test of the 18-year periodicity is the mid-cycle downturn. I had established that a ninth year recession was a repetitive syndrome of 18-year cycles. For the cycle that began in 2010, the mid-cycle low appeared in the statistics for 2019, the year before the onset of the Covid-19 pandemic (Fig. P.8).

Fig. P.9 illustrates the impact of the land cycle on the value-adding economy. Following the 2010 slump, entrepreneurs

---

26. Òscar Jordà *et al* (2019), "The Rate of Return on Everything, 1870–2015", NBER Working Paper 24112, Fig. A.9.

Figure P.8 **UK house prices and the mid-cycle downturn**

% year on year

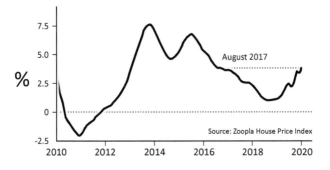

Figure P.9 **UK business incorporations ('000s)**

Quarterly business incorportaions soared during the pandemic

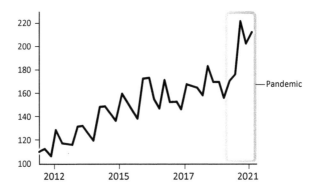

began to rebuild their businesses. There was a steady increase in the incorporation of new enterprises until 2017.[27] Then, entrepreneurship began to tail off. The risks were lower, and the capital gains from land higher, by speculating in rent-yielding assets rather than creating businesses that employ people and serve customers. Recovery, ironically, began during the pandemic lockdown.

The 18-year cycle is alive and kicking in the 21st century. In the UK, in 2017, residential land was worth £4.1 trillion. This was 76% of the total value of land, an increase from 61% in 1995. The growth of residential land value outpaced all other assets. It inflated from 21% of UK net worth in 1995 to a peak of 41% in 2007, when that burden triggered the banking crisis of 2008.

Back to the Roaring '20s

Location value is the single most revealing measure of wealth in the economy and the health of society. Economists ignore that metric in their theoretical models. That is one reason why the booms and busts are free to shred the fabric of people's lives.

If land prices terminate in 2026, the global economy has nowhere to go other than into a deep vortex. Might the pandemic of 2020 divert the cycle away from its date with The Great Bust (Box P.2)?

The best comparator was the Spanish flu of 1918-1920. That pandemic claimed the lives of at least 50 million people. The global economy shrank by about 10%. The cycle that began in 1920 turned jazz and frolics into the Roaring '20s, which ended with the mid-cycle Wall Street Crash of '29. In the UK, the flu pandemic did not deter vigorous growth of GDP. The 18-year cycle should have ended with the land price peak in 1936.

---

27. www.gov.uk/government/statistics/incorporated-companies-in-the-uk-july-to-september-2020/incorporated-companies-in-the-uk-july-to-september-2020

Box P.2 **Collision of two viruses**

In 2020, the collision of two viruses – one incubated in society, the other sourced from nature –raised the prospect of a Covid-19 global depression. Might that postpone the existential threat to the West? I could find no evidence or persuasive argument that would lead me to conclude that the pandemic-sponsored disruption of 2020 would forestall the rhythms in the world's real estate sectors.

The 18-year thesis has been tested in real time. In 1997, I offered the UK government a 10-year forecast that house prices would peak in 2007. This provided ample time for the Blair government to build defences against the depression of 2010. Blair and his chancellor, Gordon Brown, failed to erect defensive barriers. Citizens of the UK paid the price with a decade-long austerity. This episode is documented in *The Inquest*.*

* https://sharetherents.org/wp-content/uploads/2013/09/2010-The-Inquest-FINAL.pdf

---

Instead, the bust was repressed, as production in the munitions industry was ramped up. It took the prospect of a world war to rescue the economy from the late stages of the land-driven boom/bust cycle.

My prognosis for the 2020s rests on evidence from across the world. The price of land was sustained on an upward trajectory. Despite the personal and commercial tragedies caused by Covid-19, people remained fixated on house prices. In the UK, as pessimism grew about economic prospects in general, a YouGov poll revealed that most people were least concerned about house prices. Their confidence proved to be correct. House prices in 2020 soared away, with an average increase of 7.6% (the highest annual house price increase since 2016).[28] Similar trends were evident around the world, westwards to the Americas, and eastwards to Asia.

---

28. www.ons.gov.uk/economy/inflationandpriceindices/bulletins/housepriceindex/november2020

In China, under a regime that claims to favour the communal values of socialism, tax policies had actively co-opted people into becoming free riders. Salaried employees amassed portfolios of properties. Owners were not so much interested in renting out the apartments as speculating in capital gains. At the height of the pandemic, data from 70 of the biggest Chinese cities confirmed that house prices were still rising. One businessman confessed: "It's more lucrative to speculate in real estate than drug-dealing".[29]

Covid-19 killed more than four million people, but the virus from nature could be neutralised with a vaccine incubated in the laboratory. Is it too late to inoculate people against the social virus that threatens humanity itself?

Cascading crises

The biggest financial boost to the post-pandemic economy was injected on November 3, 2020. Joe Biden was elected as the 46th President of the USA. He promised to spend $2 trillion to create the Roaring '20s Mk II.

In his inaugural speech, Biden referred to six "cascading crises": Covid-19, climate change, growing inequality, racism, America's standing in the world, and the post-truth attack on democracy. His administration will fail to address these crises, because he embarked on a programme that was confined to strategies authorised by the culture of rent seeking. The US will not avoid the real estate price peak in 2026.

Scientists who study the climate crisis scatter the timing of tipping points from 2030 to 2050. Their forecasts rely on linear trends. Fallout from the rise in temperatures, for example, would proceed in a more or less straight line. The violent intrusions of nature in 2021 alarmed the experts because their models failed

---

29. Thomas Hale and Qianer Liu (2020), "China housing market shrugs off pandemic fears", *Financial Times*, August 26.

to anticipate the devastation caused by forest fires in America, droughts in Africa and the deluge of rain across Europe.

The economic implosion that follows 2026 will conflate Joe Biden's "cascading crises" into a single maelstrom. Biden, far from mitigating this event, added to its inevitability by urging OPEC, the oil-producing group of countries, to decrease prices by *increasing* the extraction of petroleum. The *Financial Times* captured the mood with this headline on August 12, 2021: *Biden to Opec: Drill, baby, drill.*

As the final dregs of vitality are squeezed out of the value-adding economy, western nations will endure an increase in the flow of desperate people from neighbouring countries. Governments, burdened by sovereign debts, will renege on their commitments to curb damage to the environment. Even before the pandemic, according to IMF estimates, the global debt – public plus private – had topped nearly $200 trillion.[30] With no "fiscal space" for manoeuvre, governments will cut back their investments in the strategies that are supposed to combat climate warming. The OECD, in its *Economic Outlook* (June 2021), predicted that the scarring inflicted by the pandemic would result in a global economy that was 3% smaller in 2026 than it would otherwise have been. By 2030, the gap would be 5.5%. Assaulted by the convergence of the existential crises, weakened governments will lack the moral and material resources to address the challenges. This was already evidence in the UK, where the government's Climate Change Committee had warned that its advice had been ignored on the need to plan for the impending catastrophes from rising seas, landslides, heatwaves, droughts and the destruction of rivers and lakes.[31]

The fallout from 2026 will strike the West like a tsunami.

30. https://blogs.imf.org/2021/02/01/the-pre-pandemic-debt-landscape-and-why-it-matters/?utm_medium=email&utm_source=govdelivery
31. www.theccc.org.uk/publication/2021-progress-report-to-parliament/

The 11ᵗʰ hour

We *can* "build back better". The fiscal vaccine would neutralise the culture of cheating. This will only happen if we all accept personal responsibility for the organic change in behaviour that is required.

Rent must replace taxes as government revenue. That would empower people to eliminate behaviour that undermines personal and social wellbeing. When pooled into the public purse, Rent actively increases productivity and employment while maximising the power of people to realise their dreams.

All of this is achieved by a pricing mechanism that conforms to the evolutionary blueprint. The Rent/revenue nexus would lay the foundations for a civilisation *sui generis*. How we can – and *must* – implement this policy is the subject of Book 2.

Electorates need to engage in conversations on how best to reconstitute the political system. Politicians must be held accountable, to end their preference for ducking and weaving around the difficult challenges. Rare is the elected office holder who admits, as did Kamala Harris, that

> The point is, when you are in public office, there really is a lot of risk associated with pursuing bold actions. Even so, I believe it is our obligation to do so. It is inherent in the oaths we take.[32]

The current variant of democracy, however, has no antidote for the insanity of rent seeking.

Correct reforms will only be authorised if people came to terms with the nature of the political power that opposes authentic democracy. Free riders remain active. In the US, led by Donald Trump and his Praetorian Guard, laws enacted in 2021 reduced the voting opportunities of millions of Americans.

To guide us in this decisive decade, I offer Book 2 as a contribution towards the development of a discipline that interrogates the causes that terminate civilisations.

---

32. Kamala Harris (2019), *The Truths We Hold*, London: Penguin, p.256.

Box P.3 **The decline of the West**

Oswald Spengler (1880–1936), a German philosopher of history, tracked the collapse of earlier civilisations over 200 years of wars and revolutions. He nominated the anti-constitutionalism of Napoleon as the starting point for the *Decline of the West*. Napoleon was Emperor of France between 1804 and 1815. Is it a coincidence that, 200 years later, the West is locked in constitutional turmoil?

► In 2019, the UK Supreme Court censured Prime Minister Boris Johnson for flouting the "unwritten" constitution.*

► In 2020, the European Union charged Poland and Hungary with abusing the "rule of law".

► In 2021, President Donald Trump was impeached for inciting the sacking of the US legislature.

Ludwig von Bertalanffy (1901–1972), a founder of general systems theory, concluded that Spengler was vindicated because

"the 'decline of the west' is not a hypothesis or a prophecy – it is an accomplished fact. That splendid cultural development which started in the European countries around the year 1000 and produced Gothic cathedrals, Renaissance art, Shakespeare and Goethe, the precise architecture of Newtonian physics and all the glory of European culture - this enormous cycle of history is accomplished and cannot be revivified by artificial means."**

By isolating the cause of the decline, we reveal the tools for resuscitating the West.

*Mark Landler (2019), "Lies, Purging and Prorogation: two Pivotal Weeks in Brexit, *New York Times*, Sept. 13. https://www.nytimes.com/2019/09/13/world/europe/brexit-johnson-parliament-bercow-churchill.html
**Ludwig von Bertalanffy (1971), *General System Theory*, London: Penguin, p.216.

A century has elapsed since Oswald Spengler wrote *The Decline of the West*. His review of the fate of earlier civilisations led to the conclusion that decline took place over a period of 200 years. For the West, his timetable ended in the first two decades of the 21st century (Box P.3).

Spengler was not crying wolf.

Neither am I.

CHAPTER ONE

2020 Evil intent

Evil stalks our world, and we can put a face to it. Donald J. Trump personifies a culture, which, if it is not contained, will destroy western civilisation. Worse, that culture now controls the means to terminate our species.

The evidence was in plain sight. But as scientists worked to combat the virus from nature, nations remained unaware that a social virus was devouring the fabric of humanity. With evil intent.

Concepts like evil, which nurture apocalyptic horrors, are dangerous. They offer refuge to shallow thinking. Emotive language diverts attention away from the root causes of existential crises.

In the past, that language did serve a purpose. People needed the catharsis that came with the use of biblical language. Apocalyptic concepts filled the voids in knowledge of how the world worked. They expressed people's intuitive sense of danger, leading to the precautionary behaviour that enabled communities to chart their way to safety.

We now have science, and the evidence from history, at our disposal. That, however, does not seem to be enough. Something is inhibiting us from challenging the culture that has taken our civilisation as hostage. It is not good enough, given the scale of the existential threats, to rely on apocalyptic language.

We need to identify, with forensic precision, the threat to humanity. The evidence is available.

It's called *free riding*.

Living on other people's backs, a way of life disguised by laws, institutions and the myths cultivated by the earliest rent seekers.

Call it an evil virus in our midst, if we must. But do not cloud the reality. The issue at stake is the social status of Rent.

When privatised, Rent is transformed into a malevolent force. Chaos follows. Ultimately, that is the reason, and no other, why the future of the West is now at stake.

Governments are failing because free riding is not held responsible for the problems it causes. It is not treated as the culture of cheating at the heart of civil society. In fact, it is celebrated. In the USA, we can put a price on that cheating. The "tax gap" is the annual sum that high-income people fail to pay into the public purse. In 2019, the gap was about $574bn.[1]

Economists treat cheating as an aberration, and they build their theoretical models accordingly. The marketplace, they claim, enforces discipline. Competition, and the pricing system, are mechanisms that encourage fair play. Wages and profits are determined by selling products to consumers. That doctrine makes no allowance for the way in which economies were tortured out of shape when rent seeking became the cultural norm.

The mind-set engineered to serve the culture of cheating contrasts with the sensibilities of earlier times. People were able to recognise free riding behaviour for what it was: a threat to the welfare of everyone in a community. That was when people lived in small groups, and it was incumbent on them to personally intervene and shame individuals who tried to live on the backs of others. With the onset of extensive urban communities, however, new strategies were required. Impersonal tools had to be devised.

---

1. https://fortune.com/2021/01/30/income-unpaid-tax-gap-2021/

- ► Authority had to be reposed in trusted individuals. First, priests. Then, princes, some of whom morphed into monarchs.

- ► Rules had to be enforced through public agencies – lawyers to write and policemen to enforce laws, courts to settle disputes.

- ► Public agencies had to be audited. Metrics were invented to ensure transparency and accountability, to prevent cheating.

In the late stages of civilisation, however, the abuse of power eroded people's control over the Rents that represented the public's revenue. That revenue was the net income that people produced and pooled for the common good. With the passage of time, understanding of the connection between Rent and wellbeing was degraded. Free riders drained the vitality from the minds of their victims, who were obliged to retreat to evocative words like *evil* to express their sense that something was wrong. Biblical language, however, does not forensically direct action to the appropriate remedial action. That explains why the signs of the revitalisation of the culture of cheating, as these surfaced within the United States, were not recognised as an existential threat.

Donald J. Trump

Donald J. Trump embodies the culture of cheating. His coarse life of material enrichment by rent seeking was crowned with the presidency of the United States of America.

Ella Kissi-Debrah personifies the victims of that culture. Rent seeking is an agent of death. It pollutes people to death. In England alone, air pollution contributes to premature deaths estimated at up to 36,000 people every year.[2] Across the globe, 7m people die prematurely every year because of practises that separate human rights from social responsibilities.[3]

The UN's Environment Programme estimates that subsidies to the worldwide energy and fossil fuel industries totalled $300bn a year. Most of those subsidies coarse through petrol pumps and surface as Rent. The subsidies are capitalised into increased share prices of the corporations that extract the fuels from the planet. To favour the rent seekers, governments inflict what the director-general of the World Health Organisation calls "the silent pandemic" on the rest of us.[4]

The danger with numbers is that they sanitize our emotions against the painful reality. On a daily basis, we engage in transactions that contribute to people's premature death. But it's not so easy to skate past those wide eyes staring out of tabloid newspapers, displaying the innocence of a child eager to pierce the future awaiting her. A child cheated by the culture that authorises free riding. Dead, in 2013, at the age of 9.

Ella lived 30 metres from the traffic which traverses London's South Circular road. A coroner ruled that she died from acute respiratory failure, severe asthma and air pollution. In her daily walks to school, she was exposed to nitrogen dioxide and particulate matter (PM) at levels that exceeded World Health Organization (WHO) guidelines. Motor vehicles emitted the killer particles into her lungs.[5] Her death was ordained by the logic of a culture that is defined by *irresponsibility*.

---

2. Public Health England (2019), Review of interventions to improve outdoor air quality and public health, p.7. www.gov.uk

3. World Health Organisation estimate. www.who.int/health-topics/air-pollution#tab=tab_1

4. Tedros Adhanom Ghebreyesus (2021), "The G20 must invest in a healthier, greener post-pandemic world", *Financial Times*, July 8.

5. www.theguardian.com/environment/2020/dec/16/girls-death-contributed-to-by-air-pollution-coroner-rules-in-landmark-case

The pricing system that was fashioned to serve rent seeking, privileged the low-cost technologies that emitted dangerous waste into the atmosphere. When inhaled, the fine particles of matter rupture people's intestines. According to Sasha Khomenko and her colleagues, if pollution was confined to the lowest measured concentrations in the 1,000 cities they studied, the annual death rate would be lower by 125,000 people.[6]

Donald Trump and little Ella are the polar opposite personalities in the drama scripted in the 16th century and enacted over the following centuries. By the artful deployment of devices of deception, the culture of cheating wrapped itself round people's minds to co-opt them into the laws and institutions that shred the living fabric out of bodies and souls.

Ella's fate was sealed by innovations that were designed to improve modes of transportation. The ever-alert free riders intruded to maximise the stream of income that surfaces as Rent. *Their culture authorised the use of cheap, and therefore dirty, technology.* Clean technologies, which capture and recycle the carbon waste, were not in their financial interests. The costs of inventing that technology would be higher, the machines more sophisticated and therefore more expensive. Those costs would leave less to pay for fossil fuels, reducing the Rent available for people who claimed to own nature's sources of energy.

► *Free riding the railways:* in the 19th century, the Rent of the coal seams occupied by the nobility was inflated because locomotive engines were not designed to capture and recycle the carbon they emitted.

► *Free riding the highways:* in the 20th century, corporations maximised Rent from petroleum because automobiles

---

6. Sasha Khomenko et al (2021), Premature mortality due to air pollution in European cities: a health impact assessment, *Lancet* Jan. 19.

were designed to emit into the atmosphere the carbon from their combustion engines.

▶ *Free riding the airwaves:* in the 21st century, digital technology transmits information, with each email adding to carbon emitted into the heavens. Because consumers do not pay the spectrum Rents into the public purse, those Rents go into the pockets of the oligarchs of Silicon Valley.

Fiscal policy is designed to maximise destruction on all fronts. Some 70% of energy-related CO_2 emissions is tax-free. The OECD reports that some of the most polluting fuels remain among the least taxed.[7] Because governments are derelict in their duty of care to their constituents, the resource Rents are channelled into private pockets.

▶ *Robber barons of the 19th century:* enriched by US government which handed free land to a few individuals to lay railway tracks, who captured the Rents from towns which sprang up along their lines.

▶ *Corporate barons of the 20th century:* their fortunes negotiated through privileged tax deals. Profits were maximised as Rents extracted via the public purse (officially called "subsidies").

▶ *Digital barons of the 21st century:* fortunes flowed from under-payment of Rent for the use of the electromagnetic spectrum. Ideological cover for the giveaway? Freedom of expression!

---

7. www.oecd-forum.org/posts/a-turning-point-for-tax-international-co-operation-for-better-regulation-of globalisation?utm_source=Adestra&utm_medium=email&utm_content=SG%20blog%20on%20tax&utm_campaign=ACI%20news%20February%202021&utm_term=gov

The narrative that imbued the collective consciousness deceived people. Capitalism was characterised as the efficient way to add value to the wealth of the nation. This ignores the fact that capitalism is composed of two distinct cultures. People who work for their living represent half of this binary arrangement. They add value to the wealth that enhances personal and social wellbeing. The other half is composed of free riding, which extracts the net income from working people. This binary aspect does not feature in the textbook definition of capitalism.

Without the aid of the rent seeking culture, Donald J. Trump would not have been able to deceive millions of people into electing him as President of the United States. He was the centurion of a culture which *had* to intervene once again in the destiny of America. That is why, when he had served his purpose, Trump was exonerated for his crimes by the highest political court of the land. He sponsored a political insurrection. He was indicted. The US Senate heard the evidence and declared him innocent. He escaped conviction because he enjoyed the protection of the culture that is the guiding hand in western civilisation.

The artistry of Donald J. Trump

Donald Trump spent decades developing the art of manipulating minds. He honed the skill while amassing Rent from real estate, he fine-tuned those skills as the host of a television show, then applied them in the quest to become the "most powerful man in the world". He claimed that he was on the side of the people who worked for their living. He promised them that, if elected as President, he would "drain the swamp" of Washington, DC: banish those who feasted on the body politic. America First.

It was all a fabrication.

Trump was the guardian of a culture which sensed it was under threat. A man of his personality had to be lodged in the White House.

To get his foot in the door, however, Trump had to create an electoral base that was devoted to him. Voters had to focus their loyalty on his personality, not a political party. He achieved this by concocting a narrative that would resonate with disgruntled middle class white people; the segment of the population whose vulnerabilities meant they could most easily be riled up with fake facts. One technique was to create an enemy. For the anxious factory workers of America, Trump presented China as the arch villain. He would "Make America Great Again" (MAGA) by imposing tariffs on products imported from China.

Blue-collar workers loved the message and flocked to hear him speak. Trump was going to revive their living standards. The figment cheered employees who had suffered a long-term decline in the take-home value of their wages. Fig. 1.1 shows what happened to the inflation-adjusted wages of employees in the

Figure 1.1 **US Wages as % of GDP**

Source: US Bureau of Economic Analysis

motor manufacturing industry. The downward spiral in purchasing power began when wages as a share of GDP peaked in 1971. Wages stood at 43% when Trump was elected.

The share allotted to rent-yielding assets exploded over this period. Trump grew ever richer from the Rents he owned or in which he held interests. Trump remained silent on the macro-economic implications. This was just another episode in the history of exploitation of people who came from the old countries of Europe, where they were dispossessed of their right to remain in their homelands.

Trump's mother was one of those people. She could not imagine a decent life, living on the western fringes of Scotland. She migrated to America in search of a better life. She married Fred Trump, who was in the business of rack-renting tenants in New York. One of his sons, Donald J., assumed the crown and built his dynasty in a career that drew him into associations with Russian oligarchs and mafia crooks. The outcome, summarised in one assessment, was this: "The Trump administration is a transnational crime syndicate masquerading as a government".[8]

The art of lying

Donald Trump lied to secure the presidency. Lies were his stock-in-trade while administering the United States of America. Vigilant journalists kept tabs: 30,573 false or misleading claims, according to the *Washington Post's* fact checkers, in the four years of his presidency.[9]

Trump conspired with autocrats to create a Kafkaesque world built on lies. One of his collaborators was President Putin. Russia's cyber-attacks on America's infrastructure went unchallenged.

---

8. Sarah Kendzior (2020), *Hiding in Plain Sight: The Invention of Donald Trump and the Erosion of America*, New York: Flatiron Books, p.176.
9. Glenn Kessler *et al* (2020), *Donald Trump and His Assault on Truth*, New York: Scribner.

It worked: add to the post-truth world by repeatedly lying, and people will believe the lies as truth. That is why, in seeking election in 2016, Trump claimed that America's unemployment rate was a hoax and that the stock market was a bubble that was about to burst. Safely inside the White House, he changed his tune and said the opposite.

The mortal implications of Trump's lies emerged during inter-views with journalist Bob Woodward. Trump confessed that, during the early stages of the Covid-19 pandemic, he deliberately deceived the American public. Trump's words were broadcast on TV: "I wanted to always play it down. I still like playing it down, because I don't want to create a panic."[10] People died because of the delay in treating the outbreak as an epidemic.[11]

China, the source of the virus, had failed to provide early warning of the outbreak in Wuhan, so Covid-19 was allowed to spread to other countries. Bob Woodward wondered: "If China was the only country to have mass infections on the scale of the 1918 pandemic, they would be at a massive economic disadvan-tage. It was a suspicion, but one held by the people who knew the regime best". What was beyond doubt was the willingness of the two most powerful men in the world – Donald Trump and Xi Jinping – to deploy lies that would cost people their lives.

The art of stealing

In its privatised form, Rent is characterised as a "transfer income". Rent seekers transfer to themselves the value created by those who produce it. In return, they give *nothing*.

---

10. Bob Woodward (2020), *Rage*, London: Simon & Schuster, p.xvii.
11. Deborah Birx, Trump's coronavirus response coordinator, estimated that most Covid-19 deaths in the US could have been prevented if Trump had acted more decisively. Her comments were offered in a CNN documentary "Covid War: The Pandemic Doctors Speak Out," aired on March 28, 2021. She referred to 450,000 avoidable deaths. www.nytimes.com/live/2021/03/28/world/covid-vaccine-coronavirus-cases

The digital age, which Trump skilfully exploited with his tweets, offered a new way to camouflage privatised Rent – *tokenisation*. The OECD acknowledged that the conversion of real estate into token forms resulted in the high volatility that "limited oversight by policy makers" which, in turn, exacerbated "the risks for investors and other market participants".[12]

Trump's wealth originated with the bequest from his father - $413m, "much of it through questionable means: loans that he had never repaid, investments in properties that had never matured; essentially gifts that had never been taxed".[13]

As President, Trump refused to comply with the convention of his predecessors. He refused to disclose his tax records. *New York Times* reporters eventually accessed the records. They revealed that Trump had paid $750 in federal income taxes the year he won the presidency, and a further $750 during his first year in the White House. True to his inclination, "He had paid no income taxes at all in 10 of the previous 15 years – largely because he reported losing much more money than he made".[14]

In a debate in 2020, Donald Trump bluntly declared that no-one pays tax "unless they are stupid". As a land speculator, Trump used tax code loopholes to minimise his tax liability to maximise his Rental income. "I don't want to pay tax," he declared. *Forbes* revealed that the self-certified expert on deal making was in debt to the tune of at least $1bn.[15]

---

12. OECD (2021), *Regulatory Approaches to the Tokenisation of Assets*, OECD Blockchain Policy Series, p.11.
13. Mary L. Trump (2020), *Too Much and Never Enough*, New York: Simon & Schuster, p.190.
14. Russ Buettner *et al* (2020), "President's taxes Long-concealed Records show Trump's Losses and Years of Tax Avoidance", *New York Times*, Sept. 27.
15. Dan Alexander (2020), "Donald Trump Has At Least $1 Billion In Debt, More Than Twice The Amount He Suggested", *Forbes*, October 16.

The narcissist personality

In the mainstream media, psychology alone was applied to diagnose Trump's personality. He was characterised as a malignant narcissist, a condition that combined narcissism with paranoia, sociopathy, and sadism.[16]

His niece, Mary L. Trump, provided insight to Trump's personality based on the knowledge of a family member who held a doctorate in psychology. She revealed how the family, starting with her grandfather, had engaged in tax dodging deals to preserve their Rent-based wealth. As for Donald, "by the late 1980s, the Trump Organization seemed to be in the business of losing money, as Donald siphoned untold millions away from Trump Management in order to support the growing myth of himself as a real estate phenom and master dealmaker". She offered this overall assessment:

> Donald today is much as he was at three years old: incapable of growing, learning, or evolving, unable to regulate his emotions, moderate his responses, or take in and synthesize information.

Mary Trump explained that her uncle was the product of a family history. She acknowledged the significance of a *New York Times* exposé published on October 2, 2018, which revealed "the long litany of potentially fraudulent and criminal activities my grandfather, aunts, and uncles had engaged in".

Trump's public *persona* concealed the ugly truth. Untold to this day is the story of how his arrival in the White House was a cultural necessity. Trump was the stooge for the culture that drives western democracies. That culture viewed the election of an African-American as president of the United States as a threat to itself. To renew itself, and reassert its sanctity,

---

16. John Gartner (2018), "DEFCON 2: Nuclear Risk Is Rising as Donald Trump Goes Downhill," in John Gartner *et al* (eds.), *Rocket Man: Nuclear Madness and the Mind of Donald Trump*, Asheville, NC: Chiron Publications, pp. 29, 30.

it needed an instrument. Donald J. Trump.

To identify the organising mechanism that steered Trump through the political hustings, we need to set the culture of free riding against the template of an authentic people-centred culture.

Authentic culture

Defensive measures are an existential necessity for free riding as a way of life. Barak Obama, as the 44th President, posed the risk of changes to public policies in ways that would diminish the spoils from rent seeking.

The reaction against Obama set in early. An alert US Department of Homeland Security warned that right-wing groups were recruiting and preparing for radical action.[17]

The United States was on course for a collision between two cultures – one authentic, the other a culture of cheating. But how do we disentangle the two?

Morality is treated as subjective in a post-truth world. This renders it difficult to know which of the rules and conventions provide *authentic* (over-riding) guidance for behaviour. Without those parameters, how do we evaluate the current state of affairs, and with confidence chart a path into the future? Do objective, authentic standards exist? What are the indicators of an authentic custom, convention or constitution?

The culture that authorises the anti-social behaviour of rent seeking actively deters initiatives that might subvert its interests. To understand the existential significance of Donald J. Trump, then, we need to recognise him as emblematic of a culture that had to strike back when America elected an African-American citizen as President.

---

17. US Department of Homeland Security (2009), *Right-wing Extremism: Current Economic and Political Climate Fueling Resurgence in Radicalization and Recruitment*, April 2009, p.4.

Authentic culture *rests on customs and practices that conform to the evolutionary blueprint that guided the emergence of humanity out of the state of nature.*[18] The key parameters of that blueprint are summarised under three headings.

▶ *Personality* Becoming human was the result of intentionally producing resources which could be invested in the psychosocial and biological assets that shaped humanity.

▶ *Property* Nature's resources were synthesised with human labour to produce Rent and renew the assets that were transmitted as the common property of future generations.

▶ *Power* Authority structures were devised to transmit the practises that enabled the earliest humans to gravitate out of nature and sustain life in increasingly complex communities.

Worldwide, people displayed variations in customs and practises that reflected the distinctive opportunities of time and place. To survive and grow, however, they had to conform to the evolutionary imperatives. This meant being

▶ *willing* to work to produce a net flow of resources: these ensured the reproduction of increasingly sophisticated cultures;

▶ *willing* to inclusively share the net flow of resources: doing so gave individuals the right of membership in society; and

▶ *willing* to adjust the administrative system to empower everyone to participate in the challenges that enriched their lives.

---

18. *#WeAreRent*, Book 1, Prologue and Ch. 1.

People who deviated from those norms imperilled themselves, which is why some groups vanished from history.

Applying these principles, we can assess whether free riding evolved a culture that qualified as authentic. If it is not authentic, we would expect our analysis to expose the flaws in current political practises. And so, by scrutinising the life and times of Donald Trump, we deepen our knowledge of the direction in which our civilisation is moving.

We need to "follow the money", to discover whether the earliest forms of rent seeking behaviour mutated into a culture *sui generis*. Does the evidence from modern history affirm the proposition that Rent, in its privatised form, constrains the power of those who oversee the laws of the land? If so, this arrangement cannot qualify as an authentic whole-of-life social formation. It detaches Rent from people who work to produce it. Political power is calibrated to suppress attempts by the dispossessed to recover their legitimate share of their community's net income. While, at all times, free riding is entirely dependent upon compliance of "the others" – the excluded. It cannot sustain itself.

The rent seeking culture is externalised from the mainstream of humanity. That detachment is imperative for a number of reasons. One would be the need to immunise the land grabbers against the consequences of their actions. Free riding rests on a *culture of cheating*, and is sustained by norms of *irresponsibility*. These characteristics offend people's ingrained moral and spiritual sensibilities, which must be dulled, enabling free riders to distance themselves from the damage they inflict on the dispossessed. One way rent seekers segregated themselves from the consequences of their behaviour was to install themselves in monumental homes behind high fences. Society divided into two universes (Box 1.1).

We can appraise the divided nature of contemporary society through the life of Donald Trump. The trauma he imprinted

---

Box 1.1 **The parallel culture**

Following the shock of the fall of Rome, a system of manorial tenure emerged across Europe. Relationships were structured around reciprocal rights attached to land, which included direct service to the monarchs. In England, this system was formalised by William's conquest in 1066. Peasants were included with secure rights to land in exchange for labour. The middle ages were not a Dark Age, as illustrated by the career of John Westwyck, a 14th century peasant. He became a monk, and undertook research in astronomy that qualified him as a scientist long before the Renaissance.*

The character of England changed in the 16th century. Henry VIII pillaged the religious life by grabbing the lands of the monasteries. Aristocrats abandoned their social responsibilities, choosing to hold land without obligation to others. The nobility extended their estates by displacing peasants from the commons. They elevated their lives into a parallel universe, a "high" culture. As a result, the vitality of the space occupied by peasants was degraded as they slumped into the low life.

* Seb Falk (2020), *The Light Ages: A Medieval Journey of Discovery*, London: Allen Lane.

---

on America is not confined to the events of January 6, 2021, when he despatched his club-wielding mob to storm the Capitol, in Washington, DC.

The Capitol, home to one of the three branches of US governance, has been sacked twice in its history. The first occasion was in 1812, when British troops set fire to the seat of American authority. The second occasion was on that day in 2021 when the 45th President incited an insurrection in his bid to retain power. Trump's fans ransacked the halls of power, seeking to capture and kill the Vice-President who had failed to do Trump's bidding. But there was more to this than a personal bid for power.

Trump was on an existential mission.

Trump's mission

Trump sought the presidency with one overriding purpose: renew the culture that underpinned the constitution of the United States. His performance must be judged against the three distinguishing characteristics of the culture of cheating.

1. *Maximisation of privatised Rent.* The national income manipulated to increase the share captured by owners of Rent-yielding assets.

2. *Monopolisation of the judiciary.* The constitution ring-fenced to exclude amendments that incorporate justice in property rights.

3. *Minimisation of government regulation.* Reduce costs of public services (funded at the expense of Rent), by diminishing people's welfare.

In his four years as President, did Donald Trump conform to these political norms of the Rent extracting culture?

Trump's tax cuts

According to the authorised narrative, capitalism is most efficient when government is confined to a small size. The financial corollary: minimised public services maximises the share of national income available as privatised Rent.

Publicly, Trump promised to clean up "the swamp" – eliminate from the corridors of power the lobbyists who sought favourable fiscal treatments for their clients. Privately, he took the swamp with him into the West Wing. He hired lobbyists to serve his administration, and lost no time in slashing taxes. In 2017, he cut taxes by $1.7bn. He claimed that, by reducing the government's revenue, he would create "good paying jobs". His adoring fans, those who had swallowed Trump's mantra *Make America Great Again*, fell for the fraud.

Trump claimed the tax cuts would be good for his supporters in the rust-belt towns. In reality, the cuts were at the expense of those people. The tax cuts elevated the value of rent-generating assets. Within two years, the US sovereign debt leapt to $22 trillion. The reciprocal consequence of the tax cuts: Republican senators demanded cuts to the medical and social security services received by people in the rust-belt towns.

In one assessment of the tax cuts, published by the IMF, Heather Boushey explained how Trump's cuts enriched the rich while starving the US of resources needed to fund public services and infrastructure. As a result, "public investment as a share of GDP…has fallen to its lowest level since 1947".[19] The tax cuts were at the expense of the welfare of the people marooned in rust-belt towns, their jobs exported to China. Steffie Woolhandler, who co-chaired *The Lancet's* Commission on Public Policy and Health in the Trump Era, noted: "Even prior to the pandemic, the United States' policies had so thoroughly failed to provide the conditions to protect health that 461,000 people who died in 2018 would have survived if our death rate were the same as other healthy nations."[20]

Under Trump's stewardship, the US national debt ended up at $27tn.

Trump's policy on tariffs was supposed to privilege domestic producers. He claimed that his tariffs would "tax the hell out of China". In fact, that tax fell on American producers and consumers at the rate of "approximately 100 percent".[21] In a tweet dated May 19, 2019, Trump claimed that his tariffs against China boosted America's GDP. "Nope," replied the *Washington Post*.

19. www.imf.org/external/pubs/ft/fandd/2020/12/how-to-make-america-more-equal-boushey.htm
20. Steffie Woolhandler *et al* (2021), Public policy and health in the Trump era, The Lancet Commission.
21. Mary Amiti *et al* (2020), Who's Paying for the US Tariffs? A Longer-Term Perspective, National Bureau of Economic Research Working Paper No. 26610.

"Tariffs reduce economic growth." The rust belt folk not only lost services that they needed from their government. They also had to pay higher prices for the goods they purchased in Main Street.

The losses inflicted by the culture of cheating were not just about dollars and cents. Since 1980, the life expectancy of U.S. citizens started to fall further behind nations like Germany. On average, Americans are three or four years behind the average life expectancy of people in France and Japan.

Channelling the US Constitution

Trump had no doubt that his mission was to safeguard the America prescribed by the Founding Fathers. In answer to a question, during an impromptu Press conference on the White House lawns, he turned his head heavenward and declared: "I am the chosen one".[22]

Trump was determined to turn his family into a dynasty of barons. To replicate the English nobility on American soil, he had to ensure that governance remained faithful to the US Constitution. The owners of land and slaves wrote that constitution. They assigned primacy to landed property.

Trump's success in shaping the judiciary became one of his legacies. He appointed three Republican lawyers to the Supreme Court, which created a 6-3 conservative majority. There was now no chance that the court would trim the constitution in ways that would undermine the culture of cheating.

One initiative failed. In his bid to override the 2020 election result, he mobilised lawyers to champion his political fraud in the courts. Some of those lawyers paid a heavy price, with one judge censuring two of them for "undermining the people's faith in our democracy and debasing the judicial process to do so".[23]

---

22. C-Span video: www.youtube.com/watch?v=lzlxrPC_E_U
23. Kiran Stacey (2021), "Trump lawyers rebuked for 'profound abuse'", *Financial Times*, August 27.

The bonfire of regulations

Advances in science and technology reduce the costs of doing business and raise the profits of enterprises. The financial gains, through competition, ultimately surface as increases in Rent.

Employees seek to share in the gains from economic efficiency through their trades unions. Because of the distortions to free enterprise caused by rent seeking, however, governments intervene with regulations on enterprises. Through one route or another, those regulations reduce the Rent flowing to free riders. To counter that prospect, conservative commentators promote the "get government off our backs" creed. They wax lyrical over the virtues of "small government". Translation: to maximise Rent, reduce government regulations. Trump acted accordingly. Ten days after moving into the White House, he signed Executive Order 13771. This was entitled "Reducing Regulation and Controlling Regulatory Costs". Trump was not interested in improving governance. He was in the business of reducing the costs of administering the affairs of state. Federal agencies were required to repeal two existing regulations for every new regulation. A bonfire of regulations followed, reducing regulatory costs by $198.6 billion in the four years of Trump's presidency.[24] That reduction inflated the net income available to rent seekers.

Mission accomplished

Donald Trump's anxiety levels need not have risen during the eight years of Barak Obama's presidency. The system was working well, as Obama confirmed when he addressed the issue of compensation for the descendants of slaves. He had considered reparations, but his power as president was insufficient to override

24. www.reginfo.gov/public/pdf/eo13771/EO_13771_Final_Accounting_for_Fiscal_Year_2020.pdf

the "politics of white resistance and resentment". What was nurturing such attitudes? Speaking on his podcast, Obama said it was "perfectly understandable why working-class white folks, middle-class white folks, folks who are having trouble paying the bills or dealing with student loans, wouldn't be too thrilled".[25]

Donald Trump's mission was to foster that discontent. In his bid for election in 2016, Trump declared with a straight face: "I have joined the political arena so that the powerful can no longer beat up on people that cannot defend themselves. *Nobody knows the system better than me*, which is why I alone can fix it. I have seen first-hand how the system is rigged against our citizens."[26] Trump serviced the culture of cheating by bamboozling the rust-belt folk into doing his bidding right up to the last day of his presidency, when his mob rioted in Washington.

Trump was, indeed, master of the art of the deal – if the art was in camouflaging his ulterior motives. He displayed his skill when he deceived those who voted for him in the first election. His base of support expanded to 74m people in the 2020 election. Some of those fans even participated in the insurrection in Washington because they believed Trump's claim that the election was rigged. They stormed and sacked the legislature. That led to Trump's second impeachment, the articles of which stated that he "wilfully made statements that, in context, encouraged – and foreseeably resulted in – lawless action at the Capitol". He "threatened the integrity of the democratic system, interfered with the peaceful transition of power, and imperilled a co-equal branch of government".

He was acquitted.

25. www.huffingtonpost.ca/entry/barack-obama-racial-slurs-race-relations-reparations
_n_60355136c5b6c0f82b48f324
26. www.politico.com/story/2016/07/full-transcript-donald-trump-nomination-accept-
ance-speech-at-rnc-225974 Emphasis added.

On April 12, 2021, the National Republican Senatorial Committee, chaired by party leader Mitch McConnell, gave its inaugural Champion for Freedom Award to Donald Trump, even as Trump was denouncing McConnell as "a dumb son of a bitch" for not overturning the election of Joe Biden as President of the USA.

Trump failed to get re-elected, but he had triumphed in his mission. America remained in safe hands. Safe, that is, for the free riders.

Democracy pivoted on a knife-edge.

2020 Countdown

Evil intent is not the force driving most free riders. They are innocent victims who work for their living, but co-opted into the culture of cheating by the "property ladder" mantra. They are vulnerable to the myths manipulated by people like Donald Trump, who fosters the idea of American greatness. Superpower status was not the result of social superiority, but scale of resources. China has now neutralised that advantage. Freedom in America now depends on equipping people with the tools for navigating the treacherous times ahead. This requires the adoption of a narrative that unites them in the common cause of humanity.

CHAPTER TWO

2021 Despair

They were sincere in their intention, to "build back better" after the pandemic. Missing was the power to deliver.

Yet...Americans elected Joe Biden as president of the most powerful country in the world! Prime Minister Boris Johnson asserted his sovereign authority by withdrawing from the European Union! What could stop them from building back better their Covid-torn communities? The answers are not located in the personalities of politicians, but in a history of state formation that originated in the 16th century. An alien culture incubated the laws and institutions of what became the democracies of the West. Free riding mutated into a way of life which, to override people's innate desire for fair play, had to fragment minds and communities. This turned into an unceasing erosion of the holistic approach to life. The current state of the world is as good as it can get. That is why the promise to "build back better" is an impossible goal.

The mechanism that organises politics remains dedicated to the private extraction of Rent. By truncating people's morals and their collective outlook on life, it became possible to enshrine that ethos in constitutions.

The rent-seeking virus was not negotiable. Universal suffrage was conditional on a structure of power that would not reverse the fundamental trends in history. That is why comprehensive audits of fiscal legislation, to assess the impact on the fabric of society, could not be authorised. By limiting accountability, lawmakers could act with impunity. Their actions were disguised as "in the public interest". This delusional form of governance became the template for modern parliamentary politics. Westminster is the archetype of that model of democracy.

The year 2021 was the tercentenary of a process that originated in the English nobility's scheme to invest in themselves the Crown's absolute power. On April 3, 1721, Robert Walpole became the first Prime Minister. The process of redefining political power progressed through to the reign of William IV (he died in 1837). The outcome was a Parliament that was hostage to the nobility. Having won the political struggle with the Crown, the contest became one between the landed class and the working class.

Industrialisation heralded a turbulent period. The working population tried to claim its fair share of the benefits of the new economic system. The nobility threw up the barricades. Their Corn Laws blocked the importation of cheaper grain from abroad. This was an existential act of self-defence. Competition from imports would have reduced food prices and raised the living standards of the working population. In doing so, however, competition would also have reduced the Rents collected by rural landlords. The Corn Laws were ultimately abolished, but only after the property owners had protected their privileges. They achieved this with a token gesture. The vote was granted to more people, but they had to meet the property qualification. The rule of rent triumphed.

The nobility reposed its political power in Parliament with the mandate to serve its vital interests. This model of governance, however, had a finite life. The dispossessed and the free riders were engaged in mortal combat. The conflict would end when cultural cannibalism, through the fiscal system, drove the body politic to destruction. I will test this thesis by interrogating Biden's promise to "build back better" after the pandemic. The evidence unfolds through a scrutiny of the tax regime and the seriously defective data on which governments based their policies.

One of the defective metrics of economic performance is GDP (gross domestic product). Governments and their economist advisors concede that GDP is an inadequate measure of welfare, but they persist in camouflaging the one metric – Rent – that would reveal the most about the state of the nation. In the US, for example, the National Income and Product Accounts "conflate 'rental income' with 'earnings,' as if all gains are 'earned.' Nothing seems to be unearned or extractive. The 'rent' category of revenue – the focus of two centuries of classical political economy – has disappeared into an Orwellian memory hole".[1] The outcome is many constitutionally unhappy people (Box 2.1).

At the US federal level, the tax code is rigged to favour the rich against low-income wage earners. This is not the *cliché* of a raging socialist, but the cool-headed conclusion of a millionaire who wrote a book called *Tax the Rich*. Morris Pearl worked with the rules from within the system. He admits that "Wealthy investors like me, a former Wall Street executive, simply should not be allowed to pick and choose when we want to pay taxes on our investments".[2]

Nonsense data camouflages the economic realities (especially the variable impacts of earned versus unearned wealth). A leading disseminator of distorted information is the US Federal Reserve,

---

1. Dirk Bezemer and Michael Hudson (2016), Finance Is Not the Economy: Reviving the Conceptual Distinction, *J of Economic Issues*, 50:3, p.749.
2. Morris Pearl (2021), "How super-rich Americans get away with paying no tax", *Financial Times*, June 15.

Box 2.1 **The delusion of Happiness**

America's GDP tripled between 1993 and 2019. Yet, over that period, the mental welfare of the people who worked to achieve that result was a national disgrace. One research project revealed that the proportion of the population in extreme distress nearly doubled to 6.4%. Among low-education midlife white people – Trump's target audience who formed his "base" – the percentage more than doubled, from 4.8% to 11.5%.

The researchers concluded that, at the personal level, the strongest predictor of extreme distress was the complaint "I am unable to work". At the state level, the strongest statistical predictor of extreme distress was a decline in manufacturing jobs.* The researchers believed that "happiness" was the true gauge of progress.** Their metric, however, does not identify a tangible tool with which law-makers can rework the social structure to empower everyone to enjoy happiness.

* David G. Blanchflower and Andrew J. Oswald (2020), Trends in Extreme Distress in the United States, 1993–2019, *American J of Public Health*.
** David G. Blanchflower and Andrew J. Oswald (2011), International Happiness, Washington, DC: NBER Working Paper 16668.

America's central bank. The way in which it compiles misleading data was analysed by Karen Petrou. She explains how, instead of serving as a steward of America's financial welfare, the Fed manipulates interest rates and analyses risks with false reasoning. This, in turn, reinforces the malign boom/bust trends in the economy.[3]

At the state level, the manipulation of tax laws to favour the owners of rent-yielding assets is painfully transparent. One blatant example is California's Proposition 13, which rigs the property tax in favour of existing homeowners.[4] A work-in-progress example is Proposition 24, which California passed in

---

3. Karen Petrou (2021), *Engine of Inequality: The Fed and the Future of Wealth in America*, Hoboken, NJ: Wiley, pp. 126-127.
4. Ted Gwartney (2016), Ch. 7 in *Rent Unmasked* (Ed: Fred Harrison), London: Shepheard-Walwyn, pp.146-149.

2020. Ostensibly, this law was intended to penalise corporations that misuse personal data extracted from their customers. Lawmakers had an ulterior motive. Part of the fines levied on the offenders would be "invested by the state with any interest or earnings sent to the state General Fund".[5] This, argues Rana Foroohar, was the creation of a sovereign wealth fund by stealth.[6] But this strategy rested on a device for raising revenue without raising taxes. The legislature would profit by accommodating bad corporate behaviour. This enabled them to avoid revising the fiscal pricing system in a way that would deter bad behaviour in the first place!

At the municipal level, the governments of towns and cities actively undermined employment prospects by offering "tax breaks" to corporations. This privileged treatment of Big Business erodes the revenue base and increases the deadweight pressures imposed on inhabitants. Infrastructure and the social services which people need are under-funded.

During Donald Trump's four years as President, his middle class fans saw the spending power of their wages deteriorate. But those who already owned their homes were enriched without having to lift a finger. The capital gains were not evenly distributed (Fig. 2.1). People who received nothing were tenant families who rented their homes. They endured a reduction in the quality of their lives: rents were increased and public services were reduced in line with the contraction in the funds flowing into the public purse.

To minimise the trauma inflicted by the tax-and-tenure nexus, palliatives are applied. These policies are funded out of taxes on earned incomes which inflict yet more stress on working people. The most vulnerable families are pushed deeper into the vortex

5. https://lao.ca.gov/BallotAnalysis/Proposition?number=24&year=2020
6. Rana Foroohar (2021), "People's capital is an idea whose time has come", *Financial Times*, June 21.

Figure 2.1 **US house price increases 2017-2020 (%)**

Change in house prices since start of Trump's term

Source: S&P/Case Shiller home price index

of despair, their communities marooned in states of disrepair. President Biden stressed this problem by highlighting the number of people whose health was damaged by lead in the 10 million service lines that pipe drinking water to American families. Biden called them a "clear and present danger to our children's health". He promised to invest $45bn in replacing the pipes, and reducing exposure to lead in 400,000 schools.[7] This was part of a multi-trillion project to upgrade the decayed infrastructure of the nation. Biden's heart was in the right place, but the biased structure of government revenue policies will ensure that he fails (Box 2.2).

Debates about the need to curtail the tax burden are carefully curated with words which accommodate the rent seeking narrative. Proposals to improve public services by increasing revenue from taxation are characterised as "raids" on incomes. Politicians are denigrated as leftists who want to "capture" people's wealth. Omitted from the conversations are references to

---

7. www.bostonglobe.com/2021/04/29/nation/why-next-100-days-will-define-biden-presidency-more-than-first-100-days/

> ## Box 2.2 **Out-of-control politics**
>
> The USA promotes itself as a rule-of-law-based democracy. One indicator of the integrity of this rule is the scale of sovereign indebtedness. The federal government has about $6 trillion in assets and $129 trillion worth of financial obligations, reports the Chicago-based non-profit Truth in Accounting. This includes $55 trillion in unfunded Medicare benefits and $41 trillion in unfunded Social Security benefits.*
>
> This is governance in which "fiscal responsibility" equates with "cut government spending". A responsible politics would equate revenue with the public services that people need. US governance is out of control. Political irresponsibility. Or (more precisely) it is a politics under the control of a culture of cheating. ATCOR reveals the winners from this form of accounting: *reduce the tax-take, and the benefits surface as increases in the value of Rent-yielding assets.*
>
> * Financial State of the Union 2021. truthinaccounting.org

personal obligations. *If everyone paid for the benefits received from public agencies, free riding would be terminated!*

How did all of this happen in the USA, a state that was constructed by colonists who declared their independence from the Mother Country when Westminster tried to tax their imported goods?

Conned by one word

The constitutional documents, which laid the foundations for the new nation-state, promoted the idea that power was reposed in "We the People…" That, Joe Biden repeatedly claimed, was the "idea" on which America was constructed.

The manipulation of one word carefully camouflaged the actual source of power. The linguistic twist was so successful that it led President Biden to make a promise that he could not keep.

He wanted to "demonstrate to our great, great grandchildren... that democracy – democracy – democracy functions and works, and together, there is nothing we can't do"?[8] The writings and actions of one English philosopher reveal the roots of the confidence trick.

It began in the 17th century when English aristocrats claimed ownership of the soil of the New World. They crafted the Fundamental Constitutions of Carolina. Eight Lords proprietors proclaimed their superior rights to most of the territory between what is now Virginia and Florida. The constitution was amended several times, but there was no tampering with the fundamental logic of the culture which they embedded in America. *Everyone was subordinate to the will of those who owned the land.*

The opening paragraph of the Carolina constitution made explicit that government was structured to "avoid erecting a numerous democracy". Anyone wanting to become a Member of Parliament had to hold at least 500 acres. Constables who enforced the law would be selected from among owners of an "estate... above a hundred acres". Freeholders alone could sit on juries. To leave no doubt about the ultimate source of power, Clause 113 obliged freeholders to pay, in silver, for each acre, "a chief rent [as] acknowledgement to the lords proprietors, their heirs and successors, forever".

John Locke was intimately involved in drafting successive versions of the Carolina constitutions. His *Two Treatises of Government* (1689/1690) went on to exercise a powerful influence on the plantation and slave owners who crafted the US Constitution a century later. Locke's philosophy, which was a key plank of the natural rights doctrine of that time, clarifies the differences between an authentic people-centred culture and a malignant ideology.

---

8. www.whitehouse.gov/briefing-room/speeches-remarks/2021/02/19/remarks-by-president-biden-at-the-2021-virtual-munich-security-conference/

In his *Treatises*, Locke argued that people were born with the right, derived from nature, to "life, liberty and estate" (Ch 7, §87). While in the state of nature, people could defend those rights. But as a result of graduating out of nature, it became incumbent on the community to enforce those inalienable rights.

That doctrine – each person's right to "life, liberty and estate" (estate being the old English term for land) – was faithfully reflected in the evolutionary blueprint that is elaborated in Book 1 of *#WeAreRent*. But did Locke really subscribe to this doctrine? His participation in the constitutions for Carolina suggest that he was not sincere.

► Slavery, he insisted, was acceptable, because it was "nothing else but the state of war continued between a lawful conqueror and a captive" (Ch 4, §24).

► Communal property could only represent 1% of total income because "ninety-nine hundredths are wholly to be put on the account of labour" (Ch 5, §40).

► Natural rights were subordinated to "a known authority, to which every one of that society may appeal…and which every one of the society ought to obey" (Ch 7, §90).

From equality of right to life, to liberty, and to land, people in Locke's world transitioned to a state where they had to obey the laws enacted by the owners of land! Thus was slavery sanctified in the New World. The aristocratic colonisers rigged the laws to favour their rent seeking behaviour. The Founding Fathers conformed to that template when they drafted the constitution in 1789. Their union eulogised the "land of the free". Well, the free who owned the land, at any rate!

How was this achieved? Landowners employed a 3-card trick to eliminate the right to land: *now you see it, now you don't!* When the

---

Box 2.3 **ATCOR and the colonies**

The British government made a costly mistake when it tried to impose taxes on the American colonies. The plantation owners understood the ATCOR effect – a tax on products sold in America would reduce the net income, the Rents which they could collect.

The Boston Tea Party rioters may not have understood the economic logic behind their opposition to taxation by Westminster. The "no taxation without representation" was sufficient to rally the crowd. But the landlords had a clear understanding of what they were doing. Land and slaves were Rent-yielding assets. That is why "Banks in the US and around the world were pouring money into Alabama, Mississippi, and Louisiana, investing in plantations, southern banks, and enslaved people, who could be mortgaged," explains Joshua D. Rothman, a professor of history at the University of Alabama.*

At the age of 10, George Washington inherited 11 slaves. While leading the revolution against the British, he enclosed as much territory as he could lay his hands on at the frontier of the New World. On securing power, he enacted the Fugitive Slave Act (1793), which he used to pursue his absconding slaves. He is now recognised as one of the richest of all of America's rich presidents.**

* Quoted in Joel K. Bourne, Jr (2020), "Cruel Commerce", *National Geographic*, February, p.52.
** Alexis Coe (2020), *You Never Forget Your First*, London: Penguin.

---

13 colonies published their Declaration of Independence on July 4, 1776, Locke's dictum of "life, liberty and estate" was converted into "life, liberty and the pursuit of happiness". The political connection to Great Britain was severed, but the ethos that animated Britain's land-grabbing aristocracy remained. The reason why the colonies ruptured their relationship with the Mother Country can be understood by the way the embedded culture of free riding is ever alert to threats that might diminish the Rent collected by landlords (Box 2.3).

Fallout in the 21st century

The claim that democratic governments can "build back better" after the pandemic can now be interrogated with the aid of the two intertwined policies of extreme concern to Joe Biden: racial prejudice and housing affordability.

Racism with a purpose

Biden wanted to equalise people's life-chances. He chose Kamala Harris, a woman of Afro-Asian heritage, as his Vice-President, and he appointed people of colour to head some of the federal agencies. Scientists supported his agenda with programmes that highlighted technology and medicine as routes to "Building a Stronger, More Sustainable U.S. Economy".[9]

On January 26, 2021, Biden signed an executive order instructing the Department of Housing and Urban Development (HUD) to pursue "fair policies". Latino and African American families were not to suffer discrimination. His order was aimed at "redressing our nation's and the Federal government's history of discriminatory housing practises and policies". The president acknowledged that federal, state, and local governments had "inhibited equal opportunity and the chance to build wealth for Black, Latino, Asian American and Pacific Islander, and Native American families, and other under-served communities". But the President could not reverse the trends of history. He was trapped in the rent seeking mind-set. He pronounced the words that would safeguard the culture of cheating: he ordained that everyone should be equally free to "build wealth" through the ownership

---

9. National Academies of Sciences Engineering Medicine (2021), "Informing the New Administration: Building a Stronger, More Sustainable U.S. Economy" Jan. 22. www. nationalacademies.org/home The proposals lacked anything that would empower the disadvantaged groups – black and white – who were segregated in the low-land-value neighbourhoods.

of housing. *Biden was reinforcing the money-grabbing technique implanted on American soil by English monarchs and the nobility.*

Everyone had the right to happiness! That happiness, however, was contingent on the ownership of land.

The source of the problem was in plain sight, but ignored.

HUD did not originate the fiscal policies that sustained racial discrimination. The legacy of political failures extended back to the Civil War of the 1860s and the emancipation of slaves on the southern plantations.

► The Ku Klux Klan was created in 1865, the year of emancipation. The lynching began. Within five years the KKK operated in all southern states to resist Reconstruction-era policies that aimed to liberate Black Americans.

► Landless whites defended themselves against economic competition from black labour by forming the National Rifle Association in 1871. Their politicians devised the filibuster, a political technique used to prevent former slaves from voting.

► Congress enacted the Fair Housing Act in 1968. Five decades later, President Biden admitted that "the racial wealth gap is wider than it was when the Fair Housing Act was enacted, driven in part by persistent disparities in access to homeownership".

Despite repeated attempts to close the gap in life-chances over the course of 50 years, segregated communities continued to endure disadvantages that exposed residents (in Biden's words) to the "burden of pollution and exposure to the impacts of climate change".

Even the election of Barak Obama, a black American, was not sufficient to undermine pathologies like racial prejudice.

There was a logic to this failure. Racial prejudice served as a lightning conductor for the white people who were also dispossessed of their share of the nation's net income, their lives prejudiced by fiscal policies that bore down hardest on people who worked for their living. Demographic divisions would continue for so long as the economics of getting rich out of the ownership of rent-yielding assets persisted. Assets like residential real estate.

For more than 200 years, the constitutional democracy had failed to treat everyone as equal. The plantation owners of the 18th century ensured that, whatever else happened, the Rent produced by the working population would go into their pockets. And so, there was not a single moment when the emancipated slaves were unshackled from the culture that brought their ancestors from Africa in the holds of British merchant ships.

So embedded was that culture that it was adopted by emancipated slaves. One of them was Henrietta Wood. She gained her freedom, but was then kidnapped and sold back into slavery to a southern plantation owner. She later sued her kidnapper. Her descendants assumed that the reparation money, $2,500, was used to purchase three residential properties.[10] The generations that followed Henrietta did prosper. But they were the exception to the rule, because extensions of the franchise in the 20th century did nothing to ease the stresses associated with homes that were not affordable for working people.

Home owners – *qua* land owners – continued to get rich while they slept, moral faculties soothed by the assurance that the capital gains were manna from heaven, not from the blood and tears of fellow citizens. Concurrently, the rooted discrimination was victimising everyone, whether they owned or rented their homes. The tax subsidy to home owners costs the U.S. Treasury between

---

10. Sydney Trent (2021), "Henrietta Wood sued for slavery reparations after the Civil War and won", *Washington Post*, Feb. 24.

$70 and $90 billion annually. About 70% of this windfall goes to households in the top 20% of the income distribution, 8% accrues to middle-income households and almost nothing to the bottom 40%.[11] Tax-funded subsidies surface in the form of higher land prices, as the OECD affirmed in its *Brick by Brick* analysis.[12]

And so, as families endured enforced idleness in the pandemic lockdowns of 2021, the land beneath their homes continued to accumulate capital gains. A two-wage family working full time for minimum wages earned less than the increase in the value of their three-bedroom home in the suburb of Dedham, on the edge of Boston, Mass.[13]

The Federal government allocates over $200 billion every year as incentives to the housing sector. About 75% goes to home owners, who on average have twice the income of renters. This contributes to the widening gap between the owners of rent-yielding assets, and those who are excluded from access to the nation's Rents. Researchers who compile the Distressed Communities Index (DCI) revealed that the longest economic expansion in U.S. history (from 2009 to 2020) had failed to benefit many communities. Spatial inequality – geographic unevenness in economic well-being – had increased during the presidency of Barak Obama. This was not the result of rational economic decision-making driven by the efficient allocation and use of resources. Nor was it due to racial prejudice. It was due to political policies that discriminated against people in low-value zip code locations, where residents failed to experience any growth in employment opportunities.[14]

11. Phillip Longman (2015), "Wealth and Generations", in Laura Choi *et al*, eds., *What It's Worth*, San Francisco: Federal Reserve Bank of San Francisco, p. 248.
12. OECD (2021), *Brick by Brick*, p.34. https://doi.org/10.1787/b453b043-en.
13. Jon Gorey (2021),"How is it that the average Boston-area house 'made' more than a minimum wage worker last year?" *Globe Magazine*, Feb. 3.
14. Kenan Fikri *et al* (2021), Uplifting America's Left Behind Places: A Roadmap for a More Equitable Economy", Washington, DC. eig.org

Figure 2.2 **Wealth Gap between White and Black Families Median family wealth ($ thousand)**

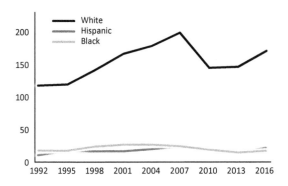

Source: Board of Governors of the Federal Reserve Board, Surveys of Consumer Finances.
https://www.federalreserve.gov/econres/scf-previous-surveys.htm

The wealth gap between rich and poor, black and white, did not close over the decades since the 1980s. The gap began to narrow after the peak in land prices in 2007, but the trend reasserted itself within three years. Fig.2.2 reveals the gap that President Biden will not close in his bid to reinforce the culture of wealth accumulation through home ownership.

Money is only one metric of the discrimination that flows from the tax-and-tenure nexus. Zip codes reveal much about the underlying structure of society. They are one window into the history of slavery, and then (after emancipation) the political machinations that preserved the free riding culture.

Housing is a key instrument for ensuring that African Americans "followed a pattern of inequality in keeping with their status in the nation".[15] Everyone suffers. Low-income families endure

---

15. Sam Fulwood III (2016), The United States' History of Segregated Housing Continues to Limit Affordable Housing, Washington, DC: Center for American Progress.

greater loss of health.[16] The San Francisco Federal Reserve estimates America's annual loss of wealth due to race and gender disparities at more than $70 trillion over the 30 years to 2019.[17]

To overcome the financial barrier to equality for all citizens, academics recommend the taxation of wealth. Their proposals are designed to fail (Box 2.4).

None of this was explained to Joe Biden. That is why, speaking on June 1, 2021, the anniversary of the Tulsa race massacre in which 300 African Americans were killed, a perplexed President noted: "Shockingly, the percentage of Black American home ownership is lower today in America than when the Fair Housing Act was passed more than 50 years ago". Biden's plans reinforce the discrimination by advocating the need to close the wealth gap by increasing the number of homes owned by black families. "Just imagine if instead of denying millions of Americans the ability to own their own home and build generational wealth, we made it possible for them to buy a home and build equity into that home and provide for their families."

The accumulation of "generational wealth" is at the expense of each succeeding generation. The process of extracting that wealth *necessarily* represses the life chances of tens of millions of Americans. One outcome is the systematic concentration of low-income families in dense neighbourhoods, the "behavioural sinks" which damage people's minds and bodies. Some of that damage emerges as anti-social behaviour.[18] The culture of deprivation feeds the Gun Law of America. According to the *New York Times*, 18,282 Americans died by lead from guns in the six months that

---

16. D.R. Williams and C. Collins (2001), Racial Residential Segregation: A Fundamental Cause of Racial Disparities in Health, *Public Health Reports*, 116 (September/October).
17. https://news.bloomberglaw.com/social-justice/fed-finds-race-gender-disparities-cut-u-s-gdp-by-2-6-trillion
18. John B. Calhoun, an ethologist at the US National Institute of Mental Health, coined the concept of "behavioural sink". See his "Population Density and Social Pathology", *Scientific American*, 1962, 206 (2).

Box 2.4 **Wealth in what?**

David Williams, a professor at the Harvard School of Public Health, traced the source of the problems associated with racial prejudice to "place". "The growth in housing equity over time is smaller for black home-owners in highly segregated areas than for owners of *comparable homes* in other areas".* The price difference was due to location values – Rent. On that basis, a general wealth tax (which fails to differentiate between earned and unearned wealth) would not equalise life-chances but it would add further deadweight losses to the economy.

Thomas Piketty, the author of *Capital in the 21st century*, championed a wealth tax for France. He estimated that governments would be able to distribute €120,000 to people at the age of 25, which "could be used, for example, as the down payment on a home".** The ATCOR impact would be immediate. Owners of existing dwellings would mop up the money by raising prices, leaving untouched the wealth disparity between renters and property owners, the landless young and the asset-rich old.

* David R. Williams and Chiquita Collins (2001), "Racial Residential Segregation: A Fundamental Cause of Racial Disparities in Health", *Public Health Reports*, 116, p.407. Emphasis added.
** L'OBS (2019), Interview with Thomas Piketty, 5 September. www.parisschoolofeconomics.eu/en/news/thomas-piketty-every-human-society-must-justify-its-inequalities/

Biden occupied the White House; 10,098 were suicides. The wounded exceeded 15,500 people. Among the dead were 275 people who were victims of 243 mass shootings.[19] The USA promotes itself as a rule-of-law-based democracy. There were 50 mass shootings in the four weeks following March 16, 2021. Gun law, however, is just one symptom of an out-of-control system.

---

19. Over the Memorial Day weekend in which Biden stressed the need to accumulate wealth through "housing", there were eight mass shootings in just 3 days. Seven people were killed and another 48 were wounded

A new paradigm?

The pandemic brought the Reagan/Thatcher era to an end.

Joe Biden was nothing, if not ambitious. He was going to create a "new paradigm". But attempts to change the political system without understanding the organising mechanism that drove the economy were doomed to disappoint. Biden's was not an authentic attempt at creating a new paradigm. He was replicating the previous initiatives which had failed. Missing was what his Vice-President called the "show the maths" technique.

Kamala Harris, in *The Truths We Hold*, explained the need to check all the steps that were taken to reach an honest answer to a problem. Biden did not apply that methodology, which is why his interventions would be no different from the FDR New Deal of the 1940s, or the Lyndon Johnson Great Society of the 1960s. Those two initiatives are celebrated for the money spent on infrastructure and improving the right of minorities to vote. They were not game-changers, however, as affirmed by the crumbling infrastructure crisis inherited by Biden. Nor did they neutralise the systemic poverty that nurtured pathological attitudes like racialism. Nor did they solve the problem of unaffordable homes.

Biden was not briefed on *why* the earlier initiatives were not sustainable. That is why he compounded the problem when he insisted, in his first address to Congress on April 27, 2021, that he would address the racial issue with his $1.8 trillion American Families Plan. The rent-seeking virus was embedded in his plan.

> [W]e have a real chance to root out systematic racism that plagues America and American lives...A chance to deliver real equity: good jobs, good schools, affordable housing, clean air, clean water, *the ability to generate wealth and pass it down to generations because you have an access to purchase a house.*[20]

20. Emphasis added.

By promoting the accumulation of wealth through land-based property, Biden reinforced the system that delivered the toxic mix of social pathologies that fragment people's lives. One family's capital gains from the ownership of a home is another family's loss. There is no win-win outcome in the scramble to free ride on other people's backs. It is mathematically impossible for everyone to be a rent seeker. The most powerful man in the world will not, because he cannot, save the most vulnerable people of America.

Despite decades spent working in Congress, Joe Biden failed to discover the fundamental flaw in the political model called "democracy". And so, from within the White House, he exported America's model of political economy to the rest of the world. His missionary was the Vice-President, Kamala Harris, who was charged with addressing the illegal migration into America.

Biden knew that migrants risking their lives to break into the US through the southern border was not a problem that could be solved by applying conventional policies. He had been down this route when he was Vice-President to Barak Obama, and he had failed. And yet, he did not commission an inquest into the reasons for that failure. Instead, he sent Kamala Harris to Guatemala in June 2021 to try and prevent the hungry, workless, landless people migrating northwards through Mexico to the Texas border.

The people of Guatemala needed a reform of the tax-and-tenure system so that they could flourish within their home communities. Instead, Harris announced a $48m donation to "support affordable housing, agri-business and enterprise". The net effect of that subsidy is the gravitational upward push in the price of land. Another consequence is yet more Guatemalans estranged from affordable homes, food and jobs, some of whom will decide to smuggle their way into the USA.

Divide and Rule

The free riding virus survives by applying the technique of "divide and rule". Nurturing racial prejudice is one such device. Prejudices do abound in western societies, but they cannot be eradicated without first being traced to their roots.

The history of slavery is cited to condemn "white culture". White traders did buy black slaves – from black Africans, who captured and sold the slaves. Christian plantation owners in America did exploit African slaves; while, in the Mediterranean, Muslim pirates kidnapped white folk to use as slaves, venturing as far as the Irish coast to plunder villages of their residents. Care in the use of language to penetrate such painful episodes is crucial.

Proxy concepts are dangerous, such as the use of race-based terms to denote low-value locations. The deployment of careless language to discuss the under-assessment of location values for property tax purposes is one example. Researchers talk about "racial and ethnic shares [as] a statistical proxy for some latent vector of factors which correlate with the assessment gap".[21] Funny language, if the implications – colouring people's minds – were not so serious.

Black low-income families are segregated in low-value locations in the US. So are white low-income families in the UK. But the repression of lifestyles did not originate in racial prejudice. The root cause of the discrimination is located in the culture of rent seeking. By failing to employ precise diagnostic language, proxy terms like "black neighbourhood" arouse baseless animosities that rupture social relationships. That diverts attention away from the source of the problems, for which there is a forensic cure. That cure was concealed from "We the people". This was achieved

---

21. Carlos Avenancio-León and Troup Howard (2020), The Assessment Gap: Racial Inequalities in Property Taxation, Washington Center for Equitable Growth, p.25. equitablegrowth.org

by constructing a political alliance centred around southern plantation owners. Heather Richardson, a professor of history at Boston College, documents that episode in history. Slave planters embedded their doctrine of property rights – over land and slaves – by building the alliance that captured the writing of the constitution in the 18th century, the construction of Republican allegiances in the 19th century, and the political conversations of the 20th century, which culminated in Ronald Reagan's election in 1980.[22]

Trump arrived to renew that programme. When he lost the presidency, the rent seeking cause was taken up by his Republicans. They successfully blocked efforts to form a bipartisan commission to investigate the assault on the Capitol. Then, in state legislatures across the country, Republicans enacted laws to keep the blocking power in the hands of those who had been co-opted by the ideology of free riding. They even wanted to exclude from children's minds the cultural context that framed the American Revolution.[23]

22. Heather Cox Richardson (2020), *How the South Won the Civil War: Oligarchy, Democracy, and the Continuing Fight for the Soul of America*, Oxford: Oxford University Press.
23. In June 2021, the Florida Board of Education explicitly ruled that schools "may not define American history as something other than the creation of a new nation based largely on universal principles stated in the Declaration of Independence". www.edweek. org/policy-politics/florida-state-board-of-education-bans-the-use-of-critical-race-theory-in-schools/2021/06

2021 Countdown

President Biden declared: "50 years from now, folks are going to look back and say, 'This was the...year and the next couple years, when America decided to win the competition of the 21st century'". But: his welfare and infrastructure policies will not divert the US from the crash of 2026. He reneged on plans to tax the super-rich. Republicans in state assemblies like Ohio rigged electoral districts to disenfranchise voters and create an undemocratic majority for Trump. Biden has just enough time to commission an investigation into the systemic violence against citizens, their communities and natural habitats.

CHAPTER THREE

2022 Silver Bullet

There is no such thing as a silver bullet. So say The Experts. By silver bullet, they mean a painless remedy to a persistent problem. Magic. That definition serves their purpose. It provides politicians with the cover for the retreat from reality. They are free to repeat the piecemeal palliatives that may not work, but which are within the comfort zones of their constituents.

One justification offered for this posture is the bogus claim that insufficient funds are available for a root-and-branch reform. This assertion goes unchallenged because social scientists treat as taboo the central problem: governments, by wilfully imposing constraints on productivity, are responsible for underfunding public services. The shortfall in finance is one consequence of the political decision not to adopt the self-funding solution.

The restoration of Rent as the public's revenue resolves socially significant problems. It does so without loading future generations with debt. Governments balance their books when they abolish the taxes that inflict deadweight losses. Productivity and quality-of-life satisfaction soar. I estimate that, for the UK, tax policies deprive the four nations of about £500bn every year. That is my central estimate. For OECD member countries, the annual losses are about $14 trillion. That is the value of how much more people would produce, once the transition to rent-as-public-revenue was completed.[1] The gains are not just of the material kind; that value represents the enhanced welfare of individuals and the rehabilitation of communities. It also reflects the benefits of a healed relationship with nature.

The Rent remedy qualifies as a silver bullet because it meets the tests of viability, comes with a proven record of accomplishment, and is comprehensive in its impact. It restores justice to the distribution of national income, by rebalancing people's rights with their responsibilities. These outcomes arise because of the restoration of integrity to the public pricing system: *the Rent people produce and pool into the public purse is proportionate to the benefits they receive.*

The symmetry of the bottom-up, organic approach – a holistic strategy – delivers the desired results. This manifests itself along three dimensions in time and space.

▶ *Decorrupting society:* by freeing people to achieve personal aspirations to the extent that they are willing to work for them. *There is no free lunch.*

▶ *Decolonising the global South:* by restoring resource Rents, millions emancipated from involuntary poverty. *The cutting edge of development.*

▶ *Decarbonising the planet:* by self-discipline, restoration of the co-evolutionary partnership with nature. *The Social Galaxy is renewed.*

A huge burden on a single policy. The OECD confirmed the policy's virtues when it analysed one of the problems that persistently defeats governments: the delivery of affordable housing

---

1. Fred Harrison (2016), Ch. 6 in *Rent Unmasked: How to Save the Global Economy and Build a Sustainable Future* (ed: Fred Harrison), London: Shepheard-Walwyn, p.126.

for everyone. It concluded: "shifting the base of [property] taxes from the value of structures to current land prices would bring multiple benefits". Those benefits included enhanced social mobility, a more efficient labour market and increased economic growth. The OECD's verdict: "Shifting [taxes] from the value of structures to current land prices would encourage construction in valuable developable areas, helping to address supply-demand mismatches".[2]

Yet, scholars conspire with lawmakers to remain silent on this policy.[3] Had the fiscal reform been adopted in time by past civilisations, they would have saved themselves from collapse. We avoid that fate by informing the public of what is at stake. Our civilisation needs a Great Reset. The conversation must begin with the issue of property rights and wrongs. The future of humanity will turn on how we perceive these rights, and on whether we are willing to correct the wrongs. The issues ought to have been resolved when European societies began to elevate themselves out of the economics of peasant farming.

► **Land** did need to be parcelled into privately held plots: to enable new forms of cultivation and capital investment.

► **Labour** did need to be specialised: new skills to increase the diversity of products that enhanced the quality of life.

► **Capital** did need to be accumulated: to increase production while relieving people and horses of heavy burdens.

---

2. OECD (2021), Brick by *Brick: Building Better Housing Policies*, Paris, p.10.
3. Honourable exceptions include James Galbraith (2016), *Inequality: What Everyone Needs to Know*, Oxford: Oxford University Press.

Increased productivity offered a richer variety of lifestyles, improved quality of food, capital formation that was sensitive to the needs of nature's habitats, and opportunities for enhanced cultural and recreational engagement. A way of life contingent on redesigning common property rights. The challenge was to realign the interface between private rights and social obligations. Property rights needed to be synchronised with a justice-based pricing system.

New forms of public services were also required, to compliment the emerging social system.

- ► Infrastructure did need to be expanded: transport and technology matching the logistical needs of commerce.

- ► Governance did need to be empowered: to negotiate the rules that deepened social relationships in urban settings.

- ► Civil services did need to be created: to enforce the contracts that laid the foundations for the new relationships.

These innovations needed resources that served the common good. The funds had to come out of net income that people jointly produced. The result would have been a resilient interface between the private and public domains. Politically, the decision-making process would have mutated into an authentic people-centred democracy, one that conformed to the evolutionary blueprint that generated the moral, material and spiritual layers of life.

In the past, people conformed to this model at critical periods in the evolution of their communities. Can we embark on such a Great Reset today?

The dynamics of power

Humanity evolved because the original social contract aligned power on terms that made possible the emergence of the Social Galaxy. Of the many stages in the evolution of that social space, the model of relevance to us is the shift away from kinship-based communities. That began 10,000 years ago. Transient hunters and herders settled down in urban environments. Facilitating this transition entailed the matching of personal rights with responsibilities. The outcome was People Power in its pure form, which enabled people to work their way to a new kind of life. Civilisation.

Specialist services were required to support dynamic, spatially riveted relationships of the extended, impersonal kind. To achieve this, people diffused some of their power to those who served administrative functions. A hierarchy of power was established. The specialists – the priests and princes and their supporting staffs – held power on a contingent basis, and they were funded out of Rent (Fig. 3.1).

Figure 3.1 **Hierarchy of Power**

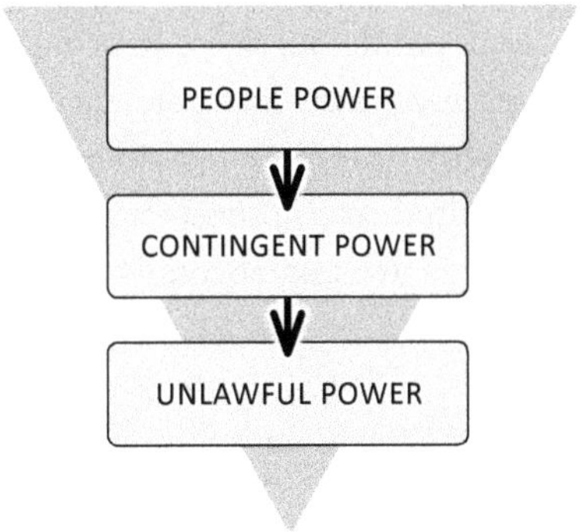

In time, a further layer of power emerged, in an unlawful form. It resulted from the dissipation of common property. Some individuals – the courtiers who walked the corridors of holy places and secular palaces - extracted some of the net income for their private use. Because of the failure to safeguard common property rights, authentic power was corrupted. In the fullness of time, deviation from the evolutionary blueprint enabled the emergence of autocrats and tyrants. They deployed violence to appropriate a larger share of Rent. They achieved this by taking control of the police power of the state. This was unlawful power in action, the exercise of which led to the replacement of Rent with taxes on private – the earned – incomes. This emasculated the authentic power of the people.

Manipulation of the kinetic power of words was one of the tactics that led to the loss of personal freedom. The route back to social sanity requires the cleansing of language, beginning with the word *tax*.

Economists have been co-opted into servicing the culture of cheating by distorting the way we think. The mind-colouring technique is subtle. For example, they refer to government revenue as flowing from "taxable income". They take for granted that earned wages and profits are the sources of public finance. In reality, Rent is the authentic source of public finance. When government collects Rent to fund public services, it is not imposing a tax. The OECD's definition of taxes lays bare the difference. Taxes, it explains, are "compulsory, unrequited payments to general government. They are unrequited in the sense that benefits provided by government to taxpayers are not normally in proportion to their payments".[4]

When Rent is pooled into the public purse, this is not a "compulsory, unrequited" act as defined by the OECD. The payment is

---

4. https://www.oecd-ilibrary.org/taxation/tax-revenue/indicator/english_d98b8cf5-en

a *price*, a *fee*, a *royalty* – call it what you will – but it is *not* a tax. *For the payment is proportionate to the benefits that people receive.* Furthermore, the payment is not compulsory. Citizens agree on the sums that they individually pay into the public purse. Government cannot arbitrarily intervene in that process of negotiation. Unrequited compulsion is absent, when an individual negotiates the level of Rent paid for exclusive possession of a given location (for residential or commercial use).

Rent unites. Taxes divide. When government draws its revenue with taxes, people lose their equal right to participate in political decision-making. Freedoms are arbitrarily constrained. Discrimination prevails, as politics severs power from common property rights and hands that power to a privileged class of people – the rent seekers.

Restoring the authenticity to power will not be easy. One reason is that the intellectual communities – academics, think tanks and special advisors to politicians – have not prepared the public for the required change in personal behaviour. Their models of the world mislead them. The scale of the wildfires, floods and droughts across the globe in 2021 shocked the scientists. Their prognoses failed to capture the speed of changes within nature. One reason for their methodological failures is their assumption that idiosyncratic individuals are primarily responsible for systemic crises. They underplay the possibility of a flaw in the structure of the social system. Hence, their rejection of a silver bullet solution to socially significant problems.

Partial analysis of problems leads to failures in governance. To save western civilisation from the risks emanating from crises such as rising global temperatures and melting ice caps, we need to "follow the money" and recover the knowledge of the root cause. That, in turn, leads us to the silver bullet remedy. Think of a rock thrown into a still pond. In nature, the ripples radiate outward. Each wave diminishes in force, the further away it gets from the original plunge of the rock. Those who curate our minds delude us into concentrating on the outer ripple, to believe that it was "caused" by the wave that came before it. In the Social Galaxy, the reverse is true (Box 3.1).

Box 3.1 **Inverting nature's square law**

The "inverse square law" is one of the forces of nature. Impacts vary according to the distance from the original cause. The further away from the source, the weaker the effect. Newton's law of universal gravitation is one example.

The reverse happens when free riders abuse the social law of Rent. Far from weakening, the ripples – the negative effects - are amplified. The initial shock is painful (as with the forced displacement of people from their traditional land holdings). In England, scores of hamlets and villages were razed to the ground to clear the line-of-sight of the landscape for landlords. Aristocratic lifestyle, anchored in monumental dwellings in privileged spaces, nurtured the modern syndrome known as NIMBY (Not in My Back Yard). Homeowners object to the construction of new dwellings, which obstruct views of the countryside and reduce the location value of their properties.

Privatised Rent pollutes the psychological, spiritual and social condition of the population. The ripples, amplified through the centuries, surface through

- ▶ *traumatic impact on the individual:* by fragmenting the population's collective consciousness;
- ▶ *the spatial reach:* local disfigurements replicated through migration to other communities;
- ▶ *the temporal sphere:* no time limit on rent seeking other than that set by its cannibalistic nature.

The pain deepens, as when successive generations find that house prices recede ever further from their reach.

Table 3.1 **Annual tax-take, England**

1066	£400,000
...and then, in the 100 years up to	
1166	£200,000
1266	£150,000
1366	£130,000
1466	£100,000
1566	£500,000
1666	£1,800,000
1791	£17,000,000

Source: Thomas Paine, *The Rights of Man*; in *Complete Works* (1885), p.408.

The Battleground

If western nations are not governed by authentic people-centred democracies, that fact should reveal itself in the fiscal statistics. Thomas Paine provided one overview (Table 3.1).

During the feudal era – the recovery phase from the collapse of Rome – kings funded themselves from the estates allocated to them for that purpose. People supported their communities with labour and goods-in-kind (usually food) – Rent in pre-monetary forms. Historians will dispute the precision of the data for the four centuries that followed William of Normandy's conquest. Not contested, however, is the downward trend. For Tom Paine, the inflection point revealed the epoch-making shift that divided the last millennium into two parts.

Something terrible happened to the character of people of England. Paine noted that, in the 400 years before the reign of Henry VIII, people in England "could not be imposed upon". They would not accept arbitrary taxation. From the accession of Henry to the throne, however, "the national character of the English has changed". After reviewing the evidence, Paine concluded that, before the 16th century, "it would have been impossible to have dragooned the former English into excess of taxation that now exists".[5]

If the folk who farmed the fields and laboured as artisans in the towns had changed, what brought this about? Intimidation. Capital punishment. Brainwashing. With the aid of the sheriff's sword, the hangman's noose, and the kinetic power of words. The slow motion 3-Act Drama was played out over three centuries.

► **Act 1: the 16th century.** Rapacious exploitation of the population as the noble land grabbers insisted that others must labour to support them.

Tom Paine analysed the theft of people's birthright. The aristocracy began to appropriate the Rents of the kingdom by enclosing the commons and using Parliament to legitimise their deeds. Parliament, he noted, was "composed entirely of men whose occupation consists in letting landed property". The Elizabethan era phased in poor laws to contain the discontent of people who were rendered rootless and consigned to a life of poverty.

► **Act 2: the 17th century.** To sustain their political power, landlords mollified labourers with tax-funded palliatives, which amplified the traumas.

Tom Paine deciphered the shift in the culture of the English. It was all to do with reducing revenue from the land tax and shifting the burden onto the products purchased by the working population. He drew attention to the injustice of the poor rates, the property tax levied by parishes on landed property to support impoverished families. The poor rates fell disproportionately on low-income households, among whom the poor lived.

5. Thomas Paine (1792), *The Rights of Man*, in *Complete Works of Thomas Paine* (1885), Chicago: Belford, Clarke, p.408.

Escaping their share of the burden were the "drones, the seraglio of males, who neither collect the honey nor form the hive, but exist only for lazy enjoyment"– their landed estates set apart from the parishes that housed the poor. They escaped the property tax burden levied to support the destitute.[6]

▶ **Act 3: the 18th century.** Tax burdens crushed productivity as the insatiable appetite of the free riders adapted England to the culture of cheating.

Poverty was endemic. Governments reduced the direct charge on Rents collected from the High and Mighty, while increasing the tax-take on labouring families.

In outward appearance, this drama is a Shakespearean tragedy. For the aristocracy, it was a tale of success. The nobility reneged on their feudal obligations and luxuriated in the life of rent seeking on the backs of fellow men and women. For the self-certified elites to survive, the institutions of civil society and the collective consciousness of the population had to be corrupted. Symptoms surfaced as dispossession, debt and despair as cultural vitality drained away.

Funding governance

The practice of politics varied in detail, according to time and place, but the function remained the same: act according to the wishes of those who controlled the net income. Variations in the Westminster and Washington models illuminate the issues. Neither institution originated with the social needs of the people, but with the wishes of those who claimed ownership of the net income. Those who control society's Rent commanded the power to design the political structures to accommodate their wishes. Westminster power was unitary, Washington was federal, but the outcomes were identical:

---

6. *Ibid*, p.405.

► **Territorial appropriation** – the 13 states of America grabbed land to the West, Britain colonised to the East.

► **Cyclical crises** – fuelled by income maldistribution, lives diminished by the pursuit of Rent privatisation.

Rent privatisation is the dynamic that colonises people's lives. If we wish to amend this arrangement, the first step is to alter the disposition of Rent. That would guide the redesign of political institutions and decision-making processes.

Political theorists define democracy as the arrangement in which every person has the right to vote in elections and appoint political representatives. The flaw in this model is revealed by the persistent failure to resolve logistically mundane problems, like ensuring the delivery of sufficient affordable homes to meet people's needs. Reformers assume that the devolution of power, with greater public participation, would yield better results. The assumption is that the "wisdom of the crowd" would lead to improved decision making. In the past, mobilising crowds did not result in happy outcomes.

Under conditions that prevail in the 21ˢᵗ century, what would it take to design a decision-making system that empowers people to solve everyday problems?

Universal suffrage is a necessary feature of an authentic form of democracy, but it is not sufficient. The mere addition of new layers of devolved political power do not deliver solutions, as illustrated by the creation of a Parliament in Scotland (see Epilogue).

In past epochs, people combined the rules handed down by the spiritual life with the customs and practises they evolved within their communities. This enabled them to align behaviour in a manner that included the freedom to accumulate and pool net income for the common good, to sustain ever-more complex social formations. The rules prescribed from within the spiritual life were used to censure irresponsible behaviour. Those rules existed "out there", independent from the material life on earth. Because of their spiritual sensibilities, people who were tempted to act as free riders could be shamed into desisting. That explains why the early free riders had to embark systematically on a strategy known as schismogenesis, the term that denotes "creation of division". To enforce the divisions, they had to eliminate sources of authority that might be invoked to censure their culture of cheating (Box 3.2).

Box 3.2 **Contorting the Social Galaxy: I**

Pre-scientific humans employed time and place as coordinates to define both realms of reality, the seen and the unseen. They expressed reality through symbols, the imagination, and moral and spiritual sensibilities. These ordered the space of objective reality for people to move through time.

Then, in the 17th century, something remarkable happened, argues Jeremy Naydler in his essays on the history of consciousness. What he calls non-locational space was erased from the collective consciousness. He attributed this to the emergence of the scientific method, which focused on the material (measurable) realm. Thus, modern astronomy's achievements were "gained at the cost of dislocating us from the spiritual universe that was the all-enveloping 'container' of the pre-modern cosmologies".*

And yet, there is no logical reason why knowledge of the outer spheres of the universe should encourage people to sacrifice the inner realms of the spiritual life. Who, then, gained from the narrowing of human consciousness? One plausible answer: those who sought to usurp the norms of justice that traditionally guided behaviour. By diminishing the (unseen) moral and spiritual realms, people were deprived of the authorities that could be used to challenge those who were abusing the traditional norms of justice. Like land grabbing.

* Jeremy Naydler (2009), *The Future of the Ancient World*, Rochester, VT: Inner Traditions, p.77.

To restore behaviour that conformed to the evolutionary blueprint, we need a clear understanding of what it means to be human. Heather Remoff, an American anthropologist and evolutionary theorist, takes the origins of our species-specific behaviour as her analytical starting point. By doing so, she was led to the conclusion that, in "a world that American economist Henry George convinces me is possible, all taxes on profit, income, sales, trade, etc. would be eliminated in favour of one that would be levied on holdings in or damage to naturally occurring resources".[7]

The evolutionary blueprint guides us to the principles of authentic democracy.

For political decision-making to conform to the binary nature of humanity – the symbiotic integration of private personas with the legacy assets inherited from earlier generations - every person must exercise the right to two votes.

► Vote 1: the *Right-to-Life vote.* The cross on the ballot records private preferences, registered in secret, free from pressure from others.

► Vote 2: the *Responsibility-for-Humanity vote.* Pooling Rent affirms commitment to the assets that constitute the fabric of human beings.

Vote 2 acknowledges personal responsibility for the community, when Rent is social in form. When Rent is privatised, however, Vote 2 becomes perverse. In France, the "double vote" law of June 29, 1820, extended a second vote to those who paid the highest taxes. The second vote translated into power that was at least three to five times as great as the voting power of those who were confined to a single vote.[8] In England, graduates of Eton (the

7. Heather Remoff (2021), *What's Sex Got To Do with It? Darwin, Love, Lust, and the Anthropocene*, London: Shepheard-Walwyn.
8. Michel Le Breton and Dominique Lepelley (2014), "An Analysis of the Electoral Law of 29 June 1820", *Revue économique*, 65(3).

Box 3.3 **Contorting the Social Galaxy: II**

Privatised Rent locks people into a pathological matrix of threats, fears and unrequited dreams.

For free riders, homes became burial monuments. The template structures were the fantastic pyramids of the late Egyptian period, just before the collapse of that civilisation. In England, from the 17th century onwards, those monuments took the form of the "county seats" of noble families, many of which had enough bedrooms to house a small army. Rental resources congealed into those monuments bear silent witness to the depletion of life in nearby hamlets, which would have otherwise flourished into villages and towns.

For those who lost their access to land, homes became prisons from which to escape by migrating to other territories.

▶ *Time is distended:* the Social Galaxy is disfigured into two layers. The nobility trace their ancestry across 10 or 15 generations (as portrayed in oil on the walls of ancestral homes). The lives of the dispossessed are limited to three generations.

▶ *Space is ruptured:* the extended expectations generated by the avarice of free riders, and the displacement of refugees seeking toeholds on other people's territories.

▶ *Minds are colonised:* egos inflated for the few, the identities and dignities of the many corroded.

Morality is degraded. Losers live by their wits. The need to survive may tempt them into anti-social behaviour. The rent seekers soothe their moral sentiments in delusions of grandeur.

sons of the aristocracy) completed their studies at Oxford and Cambridge where they were entitled to a second vote in the university constituencies. That second vote lasted from 1603 to 1950, helping to ensure that social Rent remained in private hands.

To establish an authentic democracy, we must restore the social status of Rent. Pooling that net income entails the freedom of everyone to exercise Vote 2 – to participate in the way society manages the funds for the common interest. In doing so, people adapt their behaviour to conform to the evolutionary blueprint. They do this by engaging in the market, through which they reveal their social preferences and the corresponding responsibilities. That restores power to the people on an equal basis, as they pay for the benefits they choose to receive.

The combination of Votes 1 and 2 results in the organic renewal of humane and sustainable communities.

This model of political participation could have emerged five centuries ago in Europe. It was stillborn by the feudal aristocracy. The men of noble birth could not allow authentic democracy to flourish because it conflicted with their ignoble mission. Across Europe, the nobility foredoomed the emerging civilisation to eventual failure. They seeded that failure through the tax-and-tenure model that gave them control of society's Rents. Despite the enormous growth in material prosperity from industrialisation, the existential trend was towards human degradation and social collapse (Box 3.3).

Weighing options

In grappling with whether to restore the social status of Rent, we might begin by taking into account how cities in the earliest civilisations imploded when Rent was privatised. Archaeologists excavate that story from the sand dunes of Egypt and Mesopotamia.

Rome offers the best documentation of what happens when citizens fail to neutralise free riding. By the fourth century, the oligarchs had lost control of their civilisation. The "barbarians" arrived and colonised vast tracts of the Empire with comparative ease. The migrants did not cause the collapse. Rome orchestrated its own fall, from within, by the abject failure to neutralise the culture of cheating. What happened thereafter signposts the strategies that should now be considered if we wish to prevent the collapse of western civilisation.

Europe began to recover from the fall of Rome by restoring the rural commons, with access disciplined by rules and fines. In the towns, the creation of guilds synthesised the authority of the spiritual life with the practicalities of the economic life.

> Guilds combined piety and profit because the combination helped guilds overcome free-rider problems and achieve common goals... A group mitigates free riding by forcing free riders to pay their way, or to be more exact, by establishing positive and negative inducements that align the incentives of the group and those of the individuals within it...Guilds that combined congregation and craft offered an alternative solution to their free-rider problems. That is one reason why guilds that bundled together religion and occupation were ubiquitous before the Reformation.[9]

Consensus replaced conflict. In England, however, when the feudal aristocracy began to flirt with the idea of debasing society's Rents, consensus was the last thing that they needed. They were in the business of rupturing society for their private ends. William Bulman traces the transformation from consensus to conflict through the cut-and-thrust of the 16th century, which resulted in "majoritarian political tactics" in Westminster.[10]

Driving the departure from consensus to adversarial politics was the nobility's need to redefine property rights. Leo Hollis documents that history. The transformation of land from a common resource to private property was the objective, and "new ideas of ownership were formulated and the notion of private property was sanctified as the bedrock of modern politics". The nation's destiny

9. Gary Richardson (2005), "Craft Guilds and Christianity in Late-Medieval England", *Rationality and Society*, 71, pp.141, 155, 167.
10. William J Bulman (2021), *The Rise of Majority Rule in Early Modern Britain and its Empire*, Cambridge: Cambridge University Press.

was at stake, because "whoever owned the land held the future in their hands".

> English law grew increasingly complex as it sought ways to protect land and empower landowners. This was personified in Parliament itself. And, at the start of this revolution, these tectonic shifts between power, property and privilege set up the inevitable contest between the Crown and the Commons to establish who had power over the regulation of property.[11]

The self-certified landlords won. The grotesque implications unfolded over the course of 400 years. The challenges that now confront us are epochal. Are we willing to design and implement an authentic democracy that is capable of meeting the needs of the 21st century? Or, will the culture created by the rent seekers block such reforms?

Resistance to change will be intense.

In America, Donald Trump refused to go away. He served notice of his intention when he walked out of the White House for the last time. He promised the people whom he had duped: "I look forward to continuing our incredible journey together to achieve American greatness for all of our people".

A survey by Pew Research Center conducted at the end of 2020 found that two-thirds of adults in France and the U.S., and half in the UK, believed their political system required major changes or needed to be completely reformed.[12] Across the globe, democratic politics continued the decline of 15 years in a row. Freedom House, a Washington DC-based think tank, reported that 73 countries saw their scores drop, compared to 28 which improved.[13]

To override the barriers to reform, especially the myths that were subtly foamed into people's minds, national conversations

11. Leo Hollis (2021), *Inheritance: The Lost History of Mary Davies*, London: OneWorld, p.18.

12. www.pewresearch.org/global/2021/03/31/many-in-us-western-europe-say-their-political-system-needs-major-reform/

13. https://freedomhouse.org/report/freedom-world/2021/democracy-under-siege

are needed which focus on the cultural context of the political system. Covid-19 highlighted the fault lines. The pandemic became a canary in the mine. In America, 20% of children grow up in poverty – and that was before the pandemic. Life expectancy is in decline – and that was before the pandemic. To cap it all, tens of thousands died needlessly in the pandemic because political decision-making was not fit for purpose – if that purpose is the well-being of the people. To reinforce these trends, in 2021 the Republican Party redeployed its time-honoured device in state legislatures: gerrymandering the voting system.[14]

In the UK, Dominic Cummings offered a damning indictment of democratic governance. He did so with the benefit of an insider's view of the centre of power. He worked in 10 Downing Street as chief economic adviser to Boris Johnson. He spilt the beans to a parliamentary committee.

Truth is that senior ministers, senior officials, senior advisers like me fell disastrously short of the standards that the public has a right to expect of its government in a crisis like this [the Covid pandemic]. When the public needed us most, the government failed...In any sensible, rational government, it is completely crazy that I should have been in such a senior position. It's completely crackers that someone like me should have been in there, just the same as it's crackers that Boris Johnson was in there.[15]

Cummings' hatchet job on his former boss will not escape scrutiny when the UK government's independent commission launches its investigation into the pandemic. We may assume that his confession of his own shortcomings will not be contested. He entered Downing Street as a guru of long-term forecasting and planning. He was going to improve governance by transforming the way Whitehall administered public policy. That was why I wrote to Cummings on February 24, 2020. I alerted him to

---

14. David Daley (2016), *Ratf**ked: Why Your Vote Doesn't Count*, New York: Liveright.
15. www.nytimes.com/2021/05/26/world/europe/cummings-johnson-covid.html

the land-led crash that would follow the peak in house prices in 2026. I had hoped that the long lead-time would enable him to co-ordinate research and action on the economic prospects from within Whitehall. His response was – silence. Nothing happened. He was not up to the job.

Such failures alienate the people on whose support governments rely for their votes. Missing from the corrosive cynicism people direct at politicians, however, is appreciation of why this version of democratic politics is part of the problem.

The reform agenda

The privatisation of Rent pre-dated the emergence of "capitalism", whose malevolent roots are located not in capital, but in privatised Rent.

The Covid pandemic provided the world with the opportunity for a fresh start. The virus highlighted the opportunities provided by digital technology – of working fewer hours, some of them close to home; deploying algorithms to carry much of the burden of labour; elevating productivity to fund satisfying lifestyles. If these prospects are located within an authentic democracy, societies would flourish as never before.

▶ Personal engagement in new forms of art and recreation, while participating in services rendered to others.

▶ Redesigned communities rendering neighbourhoods congenial for families occupying affordable homes.

▶ Renegotiated structures of power fit to meet the challenges of the next step forward in social evolution.

If there is any meaning to being human, it flows from the part we play in renewing, and adding to, the assets we convey to future generations. We achieve this by honouring the legacies inherited from the past generations, and by each of us working to enrich the Social Galaxy. In doing so, we stamp ourselves on that unique reality in the universe.

The majority of people today may be tempted to resist reform because they are scooping capital gains from the locations where they live and work. That self-interest, however, needs evaluation in the context of the harsh realities that prevail in the 2020s.

2022 Countdown

The prospect of Donald Trump's quest for the presidency in 2024 inspires a sense of perverse justice. He deludes his fans, America's blue-collar workers, into wanting him back in power. How would they react if their president presided as house prices peaked in 2026, with many of them losing their homes and jobs? How would he explain his failure to Make America Great Again? Under this scenario, western civilisation would have to confront The Great Convergence of existential crises with the impaired power of a humiliated President in the White House.

CHAPTER FOUR

2023 Reality

C all it the Athenian Arrogance. The ancient city claimed that its citizens were born of the earth (*autochthony*). Not so the people in other Greek cities, declared the Athenians: they were rootless, with no special relationship to the land. That doctrine rationalised a brutish practise: riding on other people's backs.

Athenians certified themselves as an epistocracy: a political system in which power is concentrated in people according to their knowledge. In reality, the rulers of Athens were dependants on the labour of others. They lived on the slaves who extracted silver from the mines of Laurion. Silver coins funded the navy that conquered other people's territories, from which the Athenians extracted Rents to fund their lavish lifestyles. The legacy to western civilisation was a model of politics that rested on a financial syndrome, which denied freedom to those who were not members of a privileged caste.

A deranged democracy

Derangement denotes a condition of inability to think clearly or behave in a controlled way, especially because of mental illness. Clinicians attribute that state to the damaged personalities of individuals. The pathology, however, also infects a society that has

---

Box 4.1 **The nature of insanity**

Dysfunctional communities may be characterised as insane when they lose the diagnostic clarity needed to identify and apply remedial policies to persistent problems. That appears to be the problem, today, in relation to challenges in the sphere of economics, as illustrated by Roger Terry's *Economic Insanity*. He laments the unequal distribution of wealth, which, he argues, offends "the American Dream". He traces people's powerlessness to deviation from the ideals of the Founding Fathers.* His critique of "capitalism", however, relies on the authorised account of the US constitution. Under that constitution, dysfunctional outcomes (like institutionalised destitution) are intentional. They result from property rights prescribed by the architects of the constitution.

Richard Giles offers a more insightful analysis of "economic insanity", which he critiques from the viewpoint of justice.** Franklin Obeng-Odoom reviewed the relationship between insanity and economics and concluded that the effective remedy was the restoration of the social status of Rent.***

* Roger Terry (1995), *Economic insanity: How growth-driven capitalism is devouring the American dream*, San Francisco, CA: Berrett-Koehler.
** Richard Giles (2019), *An Exploration of the Growth of Economic Insanity*, Sydney: Association for Good Government.
*** Franklin Obeng-Odoom (2021), "Economic Insanity", *Am. J of Econ. and Sociology*, 80(2).

---

departed from humanity's evolutionary equilibrium. The outcome is a collective form of insanity (Box 4.1).

The malaise is incubated when Rent is privatised, which begins to corrode the fabric of humanity. The deeper the penetration of privatisation, the harsher the state of derangement. If this thesis is correct, democracies as currently constituted are not fit for purpose – if that purpose is the treatment of all citizens as equals. All of the evidence points to the reality: western politics is a *faux* form of democracy. Does that explain why the democracies are beleaguered?

Political turmoil in the United States ought to serve as a warning. Consider President Biden's claim (in his Memorial Day speech on May 30, 2021), that the US was unique in the world: a nation based on an "idea". That idea is not powerful enough to ensure the future of democracy in America. The Republican Party, as the primary champion of the *status quo*, has not secured a popular majority since 1999. So, with the political Left threatening the culture of cheating, the intervention of a Trump-like character became necessary. State legislatures kept Trump's mission alive by enacting laws to empower judges to overturn future elections without evidence.[1] Discrediting the voting system inflicts a slow death on democracy.[2]

To reverse the trend towards autocracy, the democracies need to reform themselves with the aid of the authentic model of freedom. That model rests on what I call the second vote – Vote 2. Before modifying current customs and institutions, however, we need to be satisfied that *faux* democracy is no longer tenable. Does the disastrous number of political resets of the 20th century convince us that the liberal democratic model is bankrupt?

The indictment

A deranged polity would routinely display incoherent behaviour, as when actions contradict the stated objectives. A society that proclaims freedom and equality for all, but conforms to rules that divide and overrule the freedoms of large sections of the population, is not behaving in a manner consistent with its stated principles.

---

1. In the first five months of 2021, according to the Brennan Center for Justice, 48 states introduced 389 restrictive voting bills. State Voting Bills Tracker 2021 | Brennan Center for Justice
2. Steven Levitsky and Daniel Ziblatt (2019), *How Democracies Die*, London: Penguin.

An authentic democracy would not routinely limit people's freedoms. Taxes on earned incomes do restrict freedom. They are discriminatory. Taxes on entrepreneurial profits distort the allocation of resources. They curb productivity. A society that applies taxes as defined by the OECD is predatory.[3] From just these considerations on fiscal policies, we must conclude that democratic societies do not qualify as sane. Does the evidence support this proposition?

A tax-funded political system divides people into two categories. The privileged class receives benefits without paying for them. The remainder are obliged to work and pay for the services accessed by free riders.

This was the financial model bequeathed by the Athenians. The arrogance was on full display when the architects of the "Mother of Parliaments" designed their strategies for capturing the flow of Rents within the British Isles. Aristocrats were cunning, as noted by George Savile (1633–1695). He was elevated to the House of Lords in 1668 as the first Marquis of Halifax. "A Cunning Minister," he wrote, "will engage his Master to begin with a small wrong Step, which will insensibly engage him in a great one".[4] From the rent seeking point of view, each "wrong step" was in the correct direction!

► *In the 18th century:* the British nobility and their peers in America designed their constitutions to secure the privileged ownership of land.

► *In the 19th century:* landowners neutralised the masses with "crumbs off the table", such as austere workhouses to accommodate paupers.[5]

---

3. The exceptions to this rule are the few "sin taxes" which are intended to influence behaviour in favour of the goals of an authentic democracy.
4. George Savile (1912), *The Complete Works of George Savile first Marquess of Halifax*, Oxford: Clarendon Press, p.217.
5. Frances Ward and John Hainsworth (eds) (2021), *Masters and Matrons of the Llanfyllin Union Workhouse 1839-1982*, Independent Publishing Network.

▶ *In the 20ᵗʰ century:* universal suffrage became Margaret
Thatcher's "property owning democracy": people
persuaded that they earned the capital gains flowing
from their homes.

Everyone was equal before the "rule of law". Except that, in
reality, they were not. Equality was not possible because only a
proportion of the population was "of the land". The rest had no
stake in the land of their birth. They were the people denigrated
by the Athenians as barbarians.

Faux democracy foments despair. Public resources are insufficient to fund social services, and private incomes are insufficient to fund the personal needs of millions of people. All short-
falls in income are rooted in the abusive tax-and-tenure system.
Does the administration of the law support this account? In the
UK, swathes of people are vulnerable because of the incoherent
enforcement of law.

▶ *Vulnerable:* abuse of children intensified because the
tech giants protect the porn sites on their platforms.
The government refused to activate article 80(2) of the
Data Protection Act 2018. Charities could have used
that law to sue tech companies on behalf of children
whose personal information is misused.

▶ *Vulnerable:* the Equality Act (2010), §1, required public
bodies to act "in a way that is designed to reduce
the inequalities of outcome which result from socio-
economic disadvantage". Governments failed to trigger
the clause. The UN Committee on Economic, Social and
Cultural Rights censured the UK for failing in its duty
of care for its citizens.[6]

---

6. https://tbinternet.ohchr.org/_layouts/15/treatybodyexternal/SessionDetails1.
aspx?SessionID=1059&Lang=en

Politicians may be personally sincere in wanting to fulfil their duties to their electorates, but sincerity is not sufficient. Distrust of lawmakers has now mutated into a systemic crisis. As one measure of popular discontent, in the UK alone more than 700 civil society organisations are seeking to change the political system. Their proposals for reform, however, focus on the veneer rather than the substance of politics. Debates on the need for change ought to begin with agreement on the nature of people's primary needs; the reasons why those needs are unmet; and how to empower them to realise their aspirations.

The stakes are not just about personal freedom, however. Rent privatisation is compromising the contest between democracies versus autocracies. President Biden thinks that he can fend off autocracy by constructing roads and bridges. In reality, such expenditure is self-defeating under the tax-and-tenure model. Public funds invested in social infrastructure raise the location Rents that are channelled into private pockets (Box 4.2).

The failure to understand the *faux* nature of democracy exposes our world to existential threats. In America, analysts misinterpreted the reaction of the Republican Party following the exit of Trump from the White House. The party embarked on re-writing state laws to curb the voting opportunities of ethnic minorities. This behaviour was analysed as noxious to the norms upheld by American democracy. In reality, the action was a logical extension of the spirit of the constitution personified by Donald Trump. It was consistent with the values of the Founding Fathers, whose culture treated African slaves as inferior to whites (they put a number to it: blacks were worth three-fifths of whites). Under-employment is also misinterpreted as an aberration when, in reality, it is a marker of systemic success. Such misinterpretations confirm that we believe the myths that sustain the culture of cheating. People are deceived into believing that

---

Box 4.2 **Reinforcing political myths**

One political myth asserts that governments can solve the problem of unaffordable housing by cajoling construction companies into building more dwellings. This assumes that the real estate market operates like labour and capital markets: customers are satisfied when supply matches demand.

Real estate does not conform to the forces that prevail in the labour and capital markets. The most obvious difference is that land is a resource in fixed supply in places where people need to live and work. That is why political interventions intended to make homes affordable actually raise the price of land. Under prevailing tax-and-tenure laws, governments cannot match the cost of housing to the level of wages without amplifying the problem. Taxpayers' money used to fund social housing, for example, raises the deadweight burdens on taxpayers, many of whom need affordable housing.

In Canada, as house prices soared during the pandemic (hitting a 31% record high in March 2021), the Trudeau government promised to spend an additional C$3.8bn to provide 35,000 affordable dwellings. The money was intended to "help ensure that our economic recovery is an inclusive one that helps more people join the middle class".* In reality, the funds are capitalised into higher land values, which prices even more people out of the housing market.

* www.canada.ca/en/department-finance/news/2021/04/budget-2021-housing.html

---

they can correct such problems by redesigning the way they deliberate and vote from within the system that prioritises free riding.

Deconstructing democracy

Levelling up people's life chances – treating everyone as equal in terms of their rights and responsibilities – entails the *levelling out* of unearned privileges. The first step to effective reform, therefore, is to identify the junction boxes that harbour the levers of power.

The aristocracies, as the architects of the parliamentary system, were not interested in serving the interests of all citizens. Attempts to relieve distress were not acts of charity; they were defensive measures to preserve the system that generates poverty. The Poor Laws of 17th century England, for example, ensured that the pitchforks remained in the fields. Crumbs off the table were a cost worth paying to smother risks of violent reactions against injustices.

Jean-Louis de Lolme (1740–1806), a Swiss-British author, compared the Westminster model with governance on the continent. In *The Constitution of England* (1771), he repeatedly noted that ultimate power rested with Parliament because it controlled what went in and out of the public purse. This power tamed the monarchs, whose ambitions were worthless without Parliament's consent. That consent was in the form of the willingness to vote the necessary funds. Or not.

Who did Parliament represent? "The People," de Lolme repeatedly affirmed. Which people? The people who elected representatives to Parliament, of course! Those voters were owners of landed property. Land ownership was the qualification for casting a vote. Parliament was a political stitch-up! De Lolme expressed this more tactfully.

> The political rights of the people are inseparably connected with the right of property – with a right which it is as difficult to invalidate by artifice, as it is dangerous to attack by force, and which we see that the most arbitrary kings, in the full career of their power, have never offered to violate without the greatest precautions.[7]

Political power was "no more than the means of securing their property against the attempts of the Crown" to tax them. In case his readers had any doubt, de Lolme noted that taxation "forms the basis of the English constitution". His admiration for the English constitution knew no bounds. Why, he observed, "a very

---

7. J-L. de Lolme (1821), 4th edn., *The Constitution of England*, London: Wilks, p.347.

remarkable circumstance in the English government...is that spirit of extreme mildness with which justice, in criminal cases, is administered in England: a point with regard to which England differs from all other countries in the world". Extreme mildness? Really? Destitute people who committed crimes out of necessity – to keep body and soul together – were shipped to penal colonies in Australia. Out of sight, out of mind.

Evidence from the statistics

In the 16th and 17th centuries, medieval alchemy (which did not work) was replaced with an alchemy that *did* work. Reality showed up in the statistics.

For the UK, in the 1540s, after Henry VIII appropriated land that belonged to the monasteries, courtiers established the market in real estate. London's goldsmiths financed the transactions. Their rewards came in two forms. First, there was the interest charged on mortgages. Land deals entailed the capitalisation of the annual Rent into selling prices. By this means, financiers appropriated a slice of the nation's net income. Secondly, they started buying land for themselves. Thomas Calton, a City of London silversmith, was one of them. He wasted no time. In 1544, he paid Henry £609 for the Manor of Dulwich (formerly owned by Bermondsey Abbey). His grandson, Sir Francis Calton, sold the Manor in 1605 to Elizabethan actor and entrepreneur Edward Alleyn. Price: £4,900. A handsome profit of over £4,290. *Alchemy in action!*

Power was largely detached from the qualities of kingship by about 1600.[8] This created a political vacuum, which led to civil war between parliamentarians and royalists. The contest was resolved in favour of the land owning aristocracy and gentry.

8. F.A. Woods (1913), *The Influence of Monarchies: Steps to a New Science of History*, New York: Macmillan.

To function efficiently in favour of the landed classes, however, Parliament needed revenue. That revenue could come from one source only: Rent. Parliament enacted the Land Tax in 1692. This was out of fiscal necessity, not ideological preference.[9] Parliament faced an ideological conundrum: how to redesign the fiscal system to minimise the revenue collected from Rent. To achieve their goals, their lordships had to ensure that Parliament delivered the following outcomes.

▶ *Consolidate* the rent seeking culture: by reposing legislative power in the owners of land.

▶ *Facilitate* the invention of new taxes on wages, to diminish the revenue from the Land Tax.

▶ *Increase* sovereign debt: borrow to sustain budget deficits, to enable cuts in taxes on Rent.

The outcome was the predatory system constructed on the adversarial model of politics. The aristocracy and gentry captured the state. Power was distributed between landlords, financiers and the merchants who traded in natural resources. To regulate the process, power was concentrated in centralised locations (such as the bankers of Amsterdam, City of London and, eventually, Wall Street).

The gap in incomes in the 18th century reveals the success of the power grab. Joseph Massie (died 1784) compiled the data based on the taxes which people actually paid. Massie was an antiquarian who contributed to the emerging discipline of economics. He calculated the incomes and tax liabilities for selected classes of people in England (Table 4.1).

The gross disparities speak for themselves.

The nobleman who received £20,000 a year in Rent enjoyed fine living. His taxed purchases included silk, linen and

---

9. Scotland adopted a Land Tax in 1667.

Table 4.1 **Distribution of income by class: 18th century England**

Social Class and annual income	Tax liability (p.a.)
Nobleman or Gentleman: £20,000 from Rent	£6,378 18s
Nobleman or Gentleman: £10,000 from Rent	£3,197 16s
Freeholder: £100 from Rent	£30 16s
Farmer who spends £150 p.a.	£13 19s 10d
Tradesman in London who spends £300 a year	34 11d 10d
Manufacturer with wages of £31 4s p.a.	£3 2s 6d
Labourer in London with wages of £23 8s	£2 15s 3d
Husbandman/Labourer in the country, £13 p.a.	15s. 10d

foreign wines. The rural husbandman who toiled to create the nobleman's £20,000 lifestyle received an annual income of £13. His tax liability fell on essentials like salt, leather and candles.

Massie observed some of the anomalies in this fiscal regime. Taxes raised the price of goods and drove up the cost of wages. In the case of the heavy tax on "so great a necessity of life, as beer in this country", prices "give such a Wound to the British Woollen Manufactury, which is the Stay and Strength of this Nation".[10] Disputes over taxation "disturb the Repose of this Kingdom". They "proved a real Canker to the Happiness of this Nation". He appealed for honest treatment of the revenue system as "an essential Part of political Arithmetic". He illustrated the absence of honesty in "political arithmetic" with an example of the human cost: the foundling hospital. Poverty-stricken mothers resorted to the institution that received children "whose Parents could be

10. Joseph Massie (1761), *Calculations of the Present Taxes Yearly paid by a Family of Each Rank, Degree, or Class*, London, 2nd edn., pp. xii-xiii

thereby induced to wickedly and unnaturally give up and forsake them".

Shifting taxes onto the toiling labourers bumped up the cost of hiring workers. This meant that the wages of a labourer in London were twice as high as in the countryside. The London labourer did not enjoy a higher living standard compared to rural labourers. For the privilege of living in the capital city, labourers paid higher Rents.

Thomas Paine was outraged. In *The Rights of Man* he, too, highlighted the tax on beer, a tax that the aristocracy avoided because they brewed their ale on their estates.

> [W]hat will mankind think of the justice of taxation, when they know that this tax alone, from which the aristocracy are from circumstances exempt, is nearly equal to the whole of the land-tax, being in the year 1788, and it is not less now, £1,666,152, and with its proportion of the taxes on malt and hops, it exceeds it.

While poverty-stricken labourers threw themselves on the mercy of the Poor Laws, the nobility and gentlemen devoted their Rents to solving delicate problems like the dress codes and deportment that visibly signalled their aloofness from "inferior" classes. The class that self-certified itself as refined achieved this status by replacing the culture of cooperation with the self-interested doctrine grounded in conflict.[11] They soothed their consciences with the intoxicating balm of class superiority as they steadily increased the share of the nation's net income that went into their pockets. That mission continued into the 19th century and the onset of industrialisation. The outcome, two centuries later, is a quality of life in the British Isles that is far below what the nation could have achieved if, in 1799, the Pitt government had revitalised the Land Tax with Adam Smith's Annual Ground Rent. Instead, Parliament enacted the Income Tax.

---

11. Roman Krznaric (2015), *Empathy*, London: Penguin, p.6.

Figure 4.1 **The Price of Parliamentary Politics**

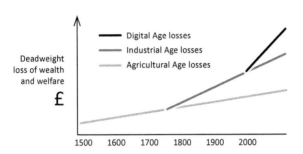

Figure 4.1 schematically evokes the trends away from social Rent to the tax-and-tenure arrangement that compromised people's lives. Originating with the destruction of the commons and the displacement of people in favour of sheep, agricultural productivity dropped below its potential. Today, productivity and personal satisfaction in rural communities would be far higher if farmers, by consent rather than coercion, had been free to adjust organically to changing technologies and consumer preferences.

Next came the dislocations in the urban-industrial sector from the late 18th century. The losses began from Day 1 of the Industrial Revolution. Investors and their employees distended their decisions in response to the fiscal burdens imposed by Parliament. The losses were in material, moral and social assets. Those losses accrued annually from then to this day. We can barely hint at the cumulative deprivation arising from the misallocation of resources stemming from interventions like the Corn Laws, which privileged the landlords.

Now, the final layer of deprivation imposed in the digital age. As spectrum Rents enrich a handful of Big Tech proprietors (who fund their excursions into outer space with society's net income), increasing numbers of people live by delivering food on scooters to families that cannot spare the time to cook their own meals. Productivity slumps while the quality-of-life gap soars.

Rescued by universal suffrage?

The onset of universal suffrage did not reverse the historical trends.

In the UK, in 1909, the House of Commons attempted to convert the public purse into a servant of the people. The House of Lords turned the thumbs down. A crisis election followed. The People's Budget enacted the Land Tax in 1910. It took just 10 years to erase that tax from the statute book. Landowners were reimbursed for the Rent they had paid into the public purse. The class-based fiscal system was safe for another 100 years. In 2021, 115 MPs earn thousands of pounds by renting out property, including 90 MPs in the governing Tory Party. Among the landlords are Prime Minister Boris Johnson and Jacob Rees-Mogg, the leader of the House of Commons.[12]

If we need further evidence of the absolute control of the rent seeking culture, consider how the democracies responded to the pandemic. Did the working population incur the cost of Covid-19? Was the value of rent-yielding assets ring-fenced? Data from the UK reveals the bias in public policies.

Nurses occupied the front line in the fight against the deadly virus. While they were placing their lives at risk, the budget of 2021 offered them a 1% increase in wages (later revised to 3%, still below the rate of inflation). The Office for Budget Responsibility forecast that, because of the scarring effects, average earnings across the economy would remain below the pre-pandemic trend all the way through to 2026.

---

12. www.opendemocracy.net/en/dark-money-investigations/quarter-tory-mps-are-private-landlords/

House prices were another story! Savills, a leading realtor, forecast that the price of buying a home would increase by 5% in 2022 and grow by 20% across the country by 2024.[13] Unlike wageworkers, the owners of rent-yielding assets were able to celebrate during the pandemic lockdown. The head of one of the UK's biggest builders noted that government action during the lockdowns had ensured that the housing market did not falter. "Is the housing market too big to fail? Particularly coming out of a pandemic with all this public debt, can prices fall? I can't contemplate that."[14] The rate of increase in "house" prices (the gains were not attributable to bricks and mortar, but to the locations) set the rhythm for the boom that would project property prices to the peak in 2026.

This land-led phenomenon was not peculiar to western democracies. In China, 70 years' worth of 5-year plans failed to command the removal of the free riding virus. The head of that autocratic regime's financial regulation agency warned that "relatively large bubbles" afflicted the property market. Real estate was the country's "greatest grey rhino in terms of financial risk".[15] Again, it is important to stress that it was the Rent extracted from locations, not the buildings, which fostered social and economic distress.

The evidence leads to a clear conclusion. Western democracies are intentionally ill-equipped to deal with the problems that blight people's lives. Parliaments confine themselves to "performative governance", which is defined as "the theatrical deployment of language, symbols, and gestures to foster an impression of good governance among citizens".[16] The cut-and-thrust of adversarial politics attracts headlines, creating the noise that shrouds the

13. www.savills.co.uk/research_articles/229130/305695-0
14. George Hammond (2021), "Housing market 'too big to fail' after stimulus", *Financial Times*, March 5.
15. Tom Mitchell (2021), "China leaders grapple with how to control rapid recovery", *Financial Times*, March 5.
16. Iza Ding (2020), "Performative Governance", *World Politics*, 72(4).

consequences of a system operating at top speed on behalf of free riding behaviour. In the US, the *Boston Globe* noted: "The point of the Senate now is not to pass lasting legislation, but stop the other party from doing anything".[17]

Societies as hostages

The "rule of law" administered by contemporary democracies turns the people of the commons into hostages. Commoners are humiliated in a thousand and one ways, their brains and emotions awash with despair. That is why they finally surrendered, becoming acolytes of the culture that captured them, a condition known as the Stockholm syndrome.[18] The doctrine of equality is ridiculed by a surfeit of evidence.

Every day, humiliation is heaped on people who work for their wages. One form of humiliation is the privileged treatment of high net worth individuals. *They recover the taxes they pay to government. This comes in the form of ever-larger annual sums bequeathed to them through the land market.* The annual increase in the value of their residential locations eclipses the sums they contribute to the public purse. In other words, *they enjoy tax-free lives.* Yet, they do not hesitate to access the public services funded by taxpayers who do not own the plots of land beneath their homes. Tenants are not reimbursed for the taxes they pay.

There is more to the fiscal swindle, however, than the varia-tions in the way the public loot is distributed. In *Ricardo's Law*, I documented the mortal risks for those who live on the wrong

---

17. James Pindell (2021), "The US Senate is structurally broken", *Boston Globe*, July 21.
18. Hong Kong offers a contemporary example of this process in action. People are being coerced into accommodating the will of the Chinese Communist Party. To protect their commercial interests, corporations are complying with intrusive laws imposed by Beijing. Schools are censuring the curriculum, to deny children access to books that would expose their minds to alternative ways of thinking and living. With time, the population that remains in the former British colony will emerge as compliant citizens under the rule of Beijing.

side of the spatial divide. I plotted UK death rates on a graph of land values. Deaths were aligned with the distribution of Rent across the economic space. People in the regions furthest from the centres of high land values endured a particularly savage deal in terms of life expectancy.[19] An average of a dozen years is lopped off the lives of babies born and raised in Drumchapel, a suburb of Glasgow, in Scotland, or in Stockton-on-Tees, in the north-east corner of England, compared to their peers born and raised in Kensington and Chelsea (London).

That insight into the spatial distribution of deaths was confirmed by the impact of Covid-19. Researchers for the Northern Health Science Alliance – which includes universities and NHS trusts – burrowed into government statistics to show how northern regions fared, compared to the rest of England. People in the north suffered a 17% higher mortality rate; a 24% higher care home mortality rate; wages fell in the north, while rising in the rest of the country; the unemployment rate was 19% higher than the rest of England. And to cap it all, the north had a larger drop in mental wellbeing and a greater rise in antidepressant prescriptions. The researchers concluded that roughly half of the increased mortality rate from COVID in the North was explained by "potentially preventable deprivation and worse pre-pandemic health".[20]

Premature death is authorised by the law of the land. Such accidents of birth – the zip code deaths – are not discussed with children in their schools, nor are they subjected to forensic study by students in universities. Which is why, through the generations, people remain helpless, defeated by the culture of cheating. Victims of the designs of rent seekers like Donald Trump, who dupe the people into doing their bidding.

---

19. Fred Harrison (2006), *Ricardo's Law: House Prices and the Great Tax Clawback Scam*, London: Shepheard-Walwyn.
20. Luke Munford *et al* (2021), A year of COVID-19 in the North: Regional inequalities in health and economic outcomes, Newcastle: Northern Health Science Alliance.

Such pathologies are a global problem, and not confined to the democracies. That reality is highlighted by unaffordable house prices. The *New York Times* surveyed the evidence.

> Market manias have an alarming record of bringing down the wider economy and of widening wealth inequality. In 484 cities around the world whose home prices are tracked by Numbeo, which compiles user-generated data about consumer prices, home prices are now beyond reach for the typical family in more than 400 of them. The least affordable U.S. city is New York, where median home prices (despite falling during the pandemic) are still more than 10 times the median annual income.[21]

No comfort can be drawn from the fact that the virus of rent seeking also blights anti-democratic regimes.

Deranged behaviour

The evidence supports the thesis that western democracies, at the cultural level, are deranged. Policies are inconsistent with proclamations. This state of affairs is existential in significance, and visible in the most elemental way. Young people are abandoning parenthood for the sake of the capital gains from real estate. Researchers in the UK have established that the rising cost of buying a home correlated with declining birth rates.[22] This is the predatory culture in its advanced stage of cannibalism.

Faux democracy survives on foundations that favour discrimination. Inequality is the name of the political game. The Johnson administration acted accordingly, when it finally decided to address

---

21. Ruchir Sharma (2020), "The Economy Is Down. Why Are Home Prices Up?" *New York Times*, Oct. 31. For a forensic examination of the empirical evidence, drawing on US data, that examines the proposition that speculation in "housing" triggers a boom that turns into a bust, see Patrick Bayer et al (2016), Speculative Fever: Investor Contagion in the Housing Bubble, National Bureau of Economic Research Working Paper 22065.
22. Valentina Tocchioni *et al* (2021), "The changing association between homeownership and the transition to parenthood", *Demography*, June 1.

the problem of people who suffer the ravages of age but cannot afford the costs of care. On September 7, 2021, the UK government announced a tax rise that would penalise young working people, to protect the Rent-generating assets of homeowners. An increase in the tax on employers and employees (called National Insurance) would raise money to fund the NHS and the care of aged citizens. Critics noted the impact: protection for the asset-rich interests of elderly people, while prejudicing the prospects of young people who were struggling to establish their families and careers. The outcome was straight out of the free rider's playbook, the existential stresses visible at all levels.

► *Biology:* short-changing the care of old folk, while forcing up house prices that cause young people to forsake parenthood.

► *Sociology:* deepening the spatial divide between North and South, with life chances distributed along the unequal Rent chain.

► *Economy:* suppressing interest rates, which drive up land values, while accommodating the ballooning national debt.

Orwellian speak was marshalled to camouflage the reality of the increased tax burden. Richi Sunak, the Chancellor of the Exchequer, claimed that the tax increase "will improve people's lives across the UK". In reality, the net gains will be absorbed as higher Rents in a process that is not a state secret: Mason Gaffney forensically documented the process in *The Losses of Nations*.[1]

Evidence of the behavioural kind affirms that modern democracies are fundamentally dis-eased. What, however, of the second

---

1. See, in particular, Mason Gaffney's "The Philosophy of Public Finance", and "An Inventory of Rent-yielding Resources" in Fred Harrison (1998), ed., *The Losses of Nations*, London: Othila Press.

feature of derangement? Do The Experts who advise govern-ments suffer from the incapacity to think straight? Consider, as an example, the justice-based need to narrow the gap between the rich and poor. Economists frame their proposals in terms of taxing "wealth". They pay little attention to whether it would be wise to distinguish between earned and unearned wealth (Box 4.3).

We need a closer evaluation of the influence of intellectuals. Are they foisting delusional visions on the post-pandemic world?

Box 4.3 **Plutocrats and the people**

Julia Cagé, an associate professor of economics at Sciences Po, in Paris, berates the "rich" who buy favourable tax treatment through their donations to political parties. These "plutocrats", she claims, shape politics. Her solution is a cap on private donations to politicians. Instead, to fund political parties, each citizen should receive a voucher worth (say) €1, to donate to the party of personal choice. That would render every citizen equal.*

The voucher, funded by taxation, would be the second vote cast by each citizen. Cagé's version of the second vote, however, accommodates the fiscal policies that prejudice the lives of citizens, and especially those on the lowest incomes. She acknowledges this shortcoming, by suggesting the reservation of some seats in parliament for "disadvan-taged socioeconomic groups". Cagé is representative of academics who promote reform without first addressing the fundamental cause of the disadvantages inflicted on people.

* Julia Cagé (2020), *The Price of Democracy*, Cambridge, MASS: Harvard University Press.

2023 Countdown

How societies implode from within is not a secret. Historians chronicled how Spain led Europe's state-sponsored rent seeking charge at the end of the 15th century, stealing a march on England. She paid the price. Gold and silver from the slave mines of the New World funded lavish lifestyles for monarchs and aristocrats. They downgraded domestic production, importing food and driving up Rents. In the 16th century, the peasants fell into debt peonage, many forced to migrate to the Americas. The free riders ignored the economic reformers known as the arbitristas. *By the 17th century, despite the inflow of bullion, Spain was no longer Europe's powerhouse. Economists and political philosophers ignore the lessons, today.*

CHAPTER FIVE

2024 Enlightenment

The conspiracy was not a theory. Rent seekers hired professors to suppress knowledge about how Rent could serve the common good.

The aim was crude: bend people's minds, by converting the science of economics into a malevolent ideology. The object was simple: enable the culture of cheating to retain control over property rights and tax policy. The conspirators triumphed.

The collective consciousness was deranged. That outcome – the mind rendered incapable of thinking straight on issues vital to the population's welfare – embedded a streak of insanity into society.

That history indicts a whole profession.

James Galbraith, a professor of economics at a university in Texas, reviewed the evidence. He traced the dishonesty of his discipline to its historical roots. Rent was expunged from economic theorising. As a result, people lost touch with the social purpose of Rent, which was supposed to fund "roads, bridges, waterworks, hospitals, schools, and the means of security. That was Ricardo's view, on behalf of the capitalists, and it would later find its most formidable proponent in the late 19th century American journalist Henry George".

Nations were divorced from reality, populations rendered ignorant, deranged, their communities distorted, governments incapable of fulfilling their duty of care.

Galbraith illustrated the material motive for rewriting classical economics with a pertinent example. In America, land was granted – free of charge – on which to establish colleges of education. Public generosity became the opportunity for private speculation.

> The land-grant universities...hired and promoted a retinue of mediocrities willing to wage a war of derision and dismissal against George's noxious creed. These were the founders of modern American economics.

A live conspiracy needs constant renewal. The professors provided that refreshment. Their economic models rested on "the belief in a transcendent celestial harmony that is at odds with the development of actual scientific thought since Charles Darwin's *The Origin of Species* appeared in 1859".[1] Detaching economics from reality disorientated the minds of generations of students. They became The Experts appointed as advisors to lawmakers.

One of the techniques for colouring people's minds (and emotions) is illustrated in *Rebellion, Rascals, and Revenue*. Michael Keen and Joel Slemrod, one a tax historian and the other a top tax expert at the IMF, acknowledged the existence of Henry George. Then they went to work on him. He was a "prophet" who displayed "messianic fervour". People who endorsed his conclusion, on the need to restore the social character of Rent, displayed "cult-like devotion", offering "evangelical support" for the policy that relieved the working population of taxes. The authors also misrepresented history. They asserted that the land tax was not enacted in Britain. It was (in 1910). They claimed that Rent as public revenue could not replace all taxes

---

1. James K. Galbraith (2021), "Dismal Economics", July 23. project-syndicate.org

(it can). And, for good measure, they failed to inform their readers of the seminal impact of the land tax on Denmark (adopted in 1926).[2]

Universities did not confine their interventions to the lecture theatres, however. They used their insider's knowledge to profitable effect. They also engaged in the land market to enrich themselves. Davarian Baldwin, a Chicago-based professor of American studies, documented the process. Universities, as charities, are relieved of fiscal obligations. That became the strategy for embarking on rent seeking by brutalising their host communities. The various techniques employed by prestigious universities to enrich themselves included the following strategies.

► *Racial segregation:* restrictive housing covenants for neighbourhoods – to elevate university-owned location values.

► *Tax exemption:* deals with governments to elevate the value of property at the expense of deficit-ridden public schools.

► *Gentrification:* sponsoring property development, which priced out residents who can no longer afford the cost of housing.

These techniques result in the "plundering of cities" as orchestrated by academic institutions, which "solidifies their political authority over housing costs, labour conditions, and policing practices for everyone living in urban America".[3]

2. Michael Keen and Joel Slemrod (2021), *Rebellion, Rascals, and Revenue*, Princeton, NJ: Princeton University Press.
3. Davarian L. Baldwin (2021), *In the Shadow of the Ivory Tower: How Universities are Plundering our Cities*, New York: Bold Type Books, p.6.

To be fair, we must acknowledge that the economics profession was not the only one co-opted into the conspiracy.[4] Economists, however, have a special responsibility. By schooling the minds of lawmakers, they influence the way a nation's income is distributed.

The social science trap

The conspiracy would not have succeeded if confined to economics. The free riders also had to hijack sociology, the emerging science of society.

Charles Darwin published *On the Origin of Species* in 1859. He employed the scientific method in his study of the evolution of life on Earth. Something changed during the next 11 years. *The Descent of Man* (1871) revealed a mind distracted by prejudices like racism and sexism.

Enter Herbert Spencer. He was working as a journalist on *The Economist* when he wrote *Social Statics* (1851). In unrestrained terms, he censured the privatisation of land. Something also changed for him in the following years. He read *On the Origin of Species* and imposed on it an interpretation that proved fatal to the development of social science.

Spencer reframed Darwin's science-based theory by summarising it in terms of "the survival of the fittest". This favoured the attitudes that served the vital interests of the landowning class. The evolutionary narrative was spun so that many scientists, including Darwin, accepted that those at the top of the class structure were the "fittest". Spencer's "social Darwinism" served an ideological purpose: the elites were worthy of their privileges because they had proved themselves fit to sit at the top of the social hierarchy.[5]

---

4. Gerald Marwell and Ruth E. Ames (1981), "Economists Free Ride, Does Anyone Else?" *J of Public Economics* (15).
5. Fred Harrison (2015), *As Evil Does* London: Geophilos, pp. 28-32.

Box 5.1 **The Descent of Man**

Darwin's sexist view of the superior status of men over women accommodated the cultural bias of the landed class. Primogeniture served the landed aristocracy. Earl Spencer, brother of Diana, Princess of Wales, provides an example. As steward of the 90-room Althorp House, he planned to leave the estate to his son, who has three older sisters. The eldest, Lady Kitty, noted: "Primogeniture can be a tricky topic". Her father was sticking with history: his English estate had served as the seat of the family for 19 generations.*

Academia is now enthusiastic about the links between biology and behavioural science, but scholars continue to focus on symptoms rather than the root cause of dysfunctional behaviour. Agustin Fuentes, a primatologist at Princeton, drawns attention to the ideological prejudices in Darwin's *The Descent of Man*. But he confines his critique to references like "Victorian and contemporary misogyny", and to "racists, sexists, and white supremacists, some of them academics".** Ironically, if they really wish to understand the origins of such perverse attitudes, academics should begin by reading the first edition of Herbert Spencer's *Social Statics*.

* Anita Singh (2021), "Daddy's old-fashioned to insist a woman won't inherit Althorp, says Lady Kitty", *Daily Telegraph*, May 13.
** Agustin Fuentes (2021), "'The Descent of Man,' 150 years on", Editorial, *Science*, May 21, 372(6544).

Spencer's perverse adaptation of evolutionary theory helped to ensure that the social sciences would not challenge the root cause of injustice. To this day, academia has been unable to reformulate Darwin in ways that would lead them back to the evolutionary blueprint that I elaborate in Book 1. Vested interests, which shaped the modern mind, shaped the terms of public discourse (Box 5.1).

Nevertheless, due largely to Henry George's book, the popular mandate for change made itself felt. This came with the Liberal Party's landslide election victory in 1906. A Land Tax was proposed in the budget of 1909, which, if it had been enacted, might have led the UK to a new kind of society. There is no doubt about what prevented this outcome. The House of Lords rejected the budget. The Liberals sought a fresh mandate from the electorate, and they returned to power in 2010. The People's Budget enacted direct charges on the nation's Rent. Land was valued and Rent collected for the public purse. It appeared as though the UK was on course for the kind of society that was consistent with the evolutionary blueprint.

Hopes evaporated in 1920. Parliament cancelled the Land Tax and reimbursed the landlords. The culture of cheating was alive and kicking. The first "build back better" of the 20th century, after World War 1, came to an ignominious end.

In the ensuing decades, contrarian voices in the economics profession were isolated. One of them was Mason Gaffney, a professor in the University of California who was frank about his predecessors:

> Neoclassical economics is the idiom of most economic discourse today. It is the paradigm that bends the twigs of young minds. Then it confines the florescence of older ones, like chicken-wire shaping a topiary. It took form about a hundred years ago, when Henry George and his reform proposals were a clear and present political danger and challenge to the landed and intellectual establishments of the world. Few people realize to what degree the founders of Neo-classical economics changed the discipline for the express purpose of deflecting George and frustrating future students seeking to follow his arguments. The stratagem was semantic: to destroy the very words in which he expressed himself.[6]

Might this history of censorship explain why, over the last 100 years, the UK led the world in a merry-go-round in public policy-making? Throughout the 20th century, economists promoted

---

6. Mason Gaffney (1994), "Neo-classical Economics as a Stratagem against Henry George", in M. Gaffney and F. Harrison (eds), *The Corruption of Economics*, London: Shepheard-Walwyn, p.29.

models that purported to explain how the world worked – or how it *ought* to work – that failed to deliver practical solutions to persistent problems. Were people like John Maynard Keynes, one of the most influential economists of the last 100 years, responsible for the catastrophes that now confront humanity? Keynes' reputation survived into the 21st century, but is that because the appraisals failed to consider how he steered himself into his world of fantasy?

Keynes anchored his thesis on governance in a worldview that intentionally brushed aside what he called "the land question". He did not explain why the land question was no longer relevant. He settled for the assertion that this transformation was the outcome of "a silent change in the facts".[7] In blocking land and Rent from his model of the economy, did the Cambridge economist steer generations of social scientists and policy makers away from the impact of privatised Rent on the fate of society?

Keynes' influence, after World War 1, was global in its reach. What might have transpired if he had thrown his weight behind fiscal rather than monetary reform? He contented himself with the proposition that governments could spend their way out of trouble. Central banks could print money to spend the economy back to full employment. By this means, by 2030 (he predicted) the working week would be down to 15 hours. In *Economic Possibilities for Our Grandchildren* Keynes foresaw a "real, permanent problem – how to use the freedom from pressing cares, how to occupy leisure time...to live wisely and agreeably and well". Carefree lifestyles had hitherto been the privilege of the rent seeking aristocracy. Keynes' characterisation of what lay in prospect for the proletariat implied that everyone would enjoy lives that were free of the discriminations caused by the private appropriation of Rent.

---

7. J.M. Keynes (1933), *Essays in Persuasion*, London: Macmillan, p.325.

The prospects of life in 2030 are a looming reality for most people alive today. For millions of people, we may anticipate longer, not shorter, working weeks. Keynes deluded himself into a false optimism. His mind-set was coloured by his dismissal of "the land question", an awkward feature of the capitalist economy that did not conveniently, and silently, slip away. But was Keynes an exception, or was his misrepresentation of reality typical of those who worked at the interface between academia and political power? To review the evidence on a manageable basis, we will chronicle the impact of one of the UK's most influential institutions, the London School of Economics (LSE).

Escape to Utopia

Covid-19 provides a setting for the framing of previous "build back better" programmes. A strategy favoured in post-pandemic academia is called Beveridge 2.0. This refers back to Beveridge 1.0, the reform plan presented to the UK after World War 2.

For the historical context we have to retreat to 1920. That was when the landlords in Parliament triumphed by cancelling the 1910 land tax. They reclaimed the Rent that they had begun to pool into the public purse (a unique event in fiscal history?). Poverty and unemployment mounted; the housing stock remained in a miserable and unaffordable condition for millions of families; the sick and elderly continued to suffer. A Labour Chancellor, Philip Snowden, made one further attempt at fiscal reform. He wrote a Land Tax into his 1931 budget. Parliament sat on it for four years before rescinding the statute.

The Depression of the 1930s, and the Second World War, inspired the idea of building-back-better. Enter that seat of radical thinking, the LSE, and a medley of distinguished professors and directors who claimed to know how to reset the economy.

For the Liberal centre:
William Beveridge (LSE Director 1919-1937)

Sir William Beveridge worked on the blueprint for post-war Britain. He highlighted the Five Great Evils – want (caused by poverty), ignorance (caused by a lack of education), squalor (caused by poor housing), idleness (caused by a lack of jobs) and disease.[8] He recommended a National Health Service (NHS) to provide universal care free at the point of delivery.

Beveridge did explore the overwhelming problem: Rent. Levels varied across the country. His statistics for 1939 affirmed David Ricardo's spatial analysis: Rent was low at the spatial margin, and grew steadily to very high levels at the economic centre. Rents imposed enormous stress on low-income families. However, instead of proposing a fiscal solution to balance life chances across the economic space, Beveridge reinforced the claims of property owners against their tenants. In the pre-war years, the vast majority of families were tenants.

Beveridge was not in the business of blaming rent seeking and speculation in the land market. The fault lay elsewhere.

> The extreme variation of rents, between regions and in the same region, for similar accommodation is evidence of failure to distribute industry and population and of failure to provide housing according to needs. No scale of social insurance benefits free from objection can be framed while the failure continues...[T]he framing of a completely satisfactory plan of social security depends on a solution of other social problems.[9]

---

8. The causal link between rent seeking and disease may not be obvious at first sight. However, scientists are now accumulating the evidence that links zoonotic diseases with habitats and human behaviour. When land grabbing degrades nature, "sick landscapes" release pathogens that mutate into human populations to create pandemics. www.newscientist.com/article/mg24933240-800-how-our-abuse-of-nature-makes-pandemics-like-covid-19-more-likely/
9. Sir William Beveridge (1942), *Social Insurance and Allied Services*, London: HMSO, pp. 80, 83, 84.

One policy only could organically resolve the evils highlighted by Beveridge. As a Liberal, he was aware of the rent-as-public-revenue policy. He flinched. As attested by the queues that lengthened outside food banks during the first two decades of the 21st century, the Welfare State failed to eliminate poverty. Similarly with the housing crisis, responsibility for which is attributed to "market failure" rather than policies that originate with government. The fatal flaw in Beveridge 1.0 was the absence of a viable revenue system for the Welfare State.

For the Socialist left:
Clement Attlee (LSE Lecturer, 1912-1923)

Clement Attlee led the Labour Party to election victory in 1945. Armed with the Beveridge Report, the Labour government created the Welfare State. Funding would come from conventional deadweight taxes. Socialist policies applied to the land market did not work.[10] Successive Labour governments failed to adopt the fiscal system that would organically eliminate poverty and the boom/bust property cycle. The socialist experiment ended in mass strikes and political chaos in the 1970s.

Fig. 5.1 traces the outcome of LSE-type interventions. The construction of socially owned housing (available at affordable rents) collapsed to near-zero levels. Tenants were driven into the private sector, where they could not afford commercial rents. Government stepped in with housing subsidies: the Rent transferred to landlords was from revenue taxed out of tenants' wages.

---

10. V.H. Blundell (1994), Flawed Land Acts 1947-1976, in Nicolaus Tideman (ed), *Land and Taxation*, London: Shepheard-Walwyn.

Figure 5.1 **The public purse as milch cow**

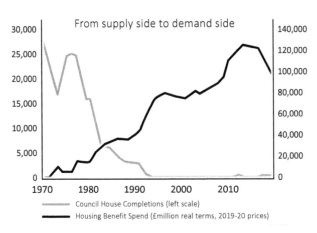

From supply side to demand side

- ⋯⋯ Council House Completions (left scale)
- ▬▬ Housing Benefit Spend (£million real terms, 2019-20 prices)

For the Conservative right:
F.A. Hayek (LSE Professor, 1931-1950)

Friedrich von Hayek laid the foundations for the application of the post-classical model of economics in the Thatcher/Reagan era. He shaped the Chicago School doctrines that became influential around the world.

In 1959, Hayek authored the terms for a constitution of liberty. He acknowledged the virtues of Rent as public revenue. There was, however – he insisted - a practical problem: the difficulty of distinguishing between the values created by nature and society from the value created by the individual. "Though we might often wish that things were as simple as the single-tax program assumes, we will find in it no solution to any of the problems with which we are concerned."[11]

11. F.A. Hayek (1960), London: Routledge & Kegan Paul, *The Constitution of Liberty*, p.353.

Academics like Hayek repeatedly cite the issue of valuing land to side-line Rent as the nation's revenue base. They ignore the empirical evidence, such as what happened in Scotland after the enactment of the People's Budget in 1910. It took just five years for the newly formed Valuation Office to value 99.7% of the land.[12] The surveyors achieved this feat with pencil and paper. Imagine how much quicker they could have compiled their register of location rents with the aid of satellite photography and computer power.

Left and Right failed. Would a middle-of-the-road reset provide a sustainable solution?

For the Third Way:
Anthony Giddens (LSE Director, 1997-2003)

Giddens published *The Third Way* in 1998. Social democratic politicians, including Bill Clinton and Tony Blair, welcomed his version of egalitarian politics.

The present author warned Blair in 1997 that house prices would peak in 2007, triggering a depression. Blair failed to act. He resigned in 2007, after 10 years in Downing Street. The sub-prime mortgage scam exploded in 2008. Blair bequeathed the financial fall-out to his chancellor, Gordon Brown, and went off to create a multi-million pound property portfolio for his family.[13] Ten years later, in 2017, Tony Blair's Institute for Global Change advertised land value taxation as a fairer way to solve the housing crisis.[14] Too late: Blair was no longer shaping the nation's fiscal policy, and the UK was enduring his legacy, the political paralysis known as austerity.

---

12. https://webarchive.nrscotland.gov.uk/20170203093936/https://www.nrscotland.gov.uk/node/2005
13. www.nationalrentersalliance.co.uk/news/landlord/tony-blair-sets-buy-let-property-company-avoid-tax-rises/
14. www.mortgagestrategy.co.uk/news/tony-blair-backs-land-value-tax-crack-housing-crisis/

Back to Beveridge:
Minouche Shafik (LSE Director, 2017–)

"And so here we are again, in need of a new paradigm," wrote Baroness Shafik in a book that promoted the need for a new social contract.[15] Her *curriculum vitae* qualified her as an Expert: Vice President of the World Bank, Deputy Managing Director of the IMF, Deputy Governor of the Bank of England, and Permanent Secretary at the UK's Department for International Development. She was elevated into the House of Lords in 2020.

When she arrived at the LSE, Shafik launched a programme of research called Beveridge 2.0. Her book reassured readers that the world was on "a direction of travel that is economically feasible". The baroness drew comfort from the statistics on poverty. In recent decades, millions of people had emerged out of poverty. The fact that millions were earning a dollar a day more than 20 years ago, however, was not due to philosophical, political or academic enlightenment. Under pressure from their previous failures, Asian governments eased their command over their economies. Greater freedom enabled people to raise their productivity. Offsetting those gains was the deepening of the existential crises. With the passage of every day, the prospects of reversing the trends that threaten the resilience of the Social Galaxy grow ever dimmer. There is nothing in Beveridge 2.0 to reverse those trends.

Do we need to get back to basics?

The Land Question Revisited

Brett Christophers is a professor in the Department of Social and Economic Geography at Uppsala University. In *Rentier Capitalism*, he spotlights the corporations that deploy monopoly power to collect super-profits. By curbing competition, and doing

---

15. Minouche Shafik (2021), *What We Owe Each Other*, London: Bodley Head, p.xiv.

backroom deals with politicians, they skew market prices to their advantage. That model, he says, prevailed between 1980 and 2020, thanks to Margaret Thatcher's privatisation of public land.

According to Christophers, one consequence was the termination of the study of land economics. Doreen Massey (1944-2016), an academic who specialised in Marxist geography, was one victim. She was working at the London-based Centre for Environmental Studies during the 1970s when

> The Thatcher government withdrew funding before 1979 was out. What had been a virtuous circle soon became a vicious one. Driving landownership off the political agenda helped drive it off the academic agenda: despite its being among her most original and brilliant contributions, Massey's work on landownership has largely sunk without trace.

Academics were not the only victims.

> Equally, driving landownership off the academic agenda helped drive it off the political agenda; people have failed to protest land privatisation because, despite the enormous scale of the programme, it has never since been a politically visible issue.[16]

Brett Christophers' characterisation of history is troubling. As an academic, he ought to have known that a gaping hole in the study of land and Rent did not arise during those 40 years. Some scholars were vigorously charting the impact of the tax-and-tenure nexus on the body politic. In the United States alone,

▶ Mason Gaffney undertook outstanding research into the economics of land ownership, and the implications for public policy.[17]

---

16. Brett Christophers (2019), *The New Enclosure*, London: Verso, p.329.
17. Gaffney's work was curated by Prof. Mary M. Cleveland and is available on https://masongaffney.org/

▶ Nobel laureate William Vickrey, at Columbia University, explained how to fund mass transit systems out of location values.[18]

▶ Nicolaus Tideman explained that Rent-as-public-revenue was better than neutral: it delivered efficiencies to everyone's benefit.[19]

Other academics who worked in this field included Fred Foldvary and Kris Feder in the USA; in the UK, professors at the Universities of Strathclyde (Roger Sandilands) and Oxford (John Muellbauer); and in Germany, Dirk Löhr not only taught economics at his university, he helped to secure Rent-based fiscal reform in the German state of Baden-Württemberg.

The work of the professors during the past four decades was supported by powerful research undertaken by others. In the UK, the impact of land privatisation was forensically analysed by a High Court judge (Sir Kenneth Jupp MC), an epidemiologist (Professor G.J. Miller) and a university lecturer in animal biology who became a land-owning farmer (Dr Duncan Pickard). Working alongside them were property specialists. Edward Dodson (USA) applied his knowledge to inform his colleagues in Fannie Mae, the government sponsored mortgage enterprise. Peter Meakin (South Africa) canvassed the need to reinterpret the post-apartheid constitution, which had failed to deliver justice to shantytown residents. Bryan Kavanagh (Australia) applied his insights as a realtor to compile statistics charting the decline in Rents collected by governments over the course of the 20th century.

---

18. See, for example, William Vickrey (1995), Propositions Relating to Site Value Taxation, paper presented at a TRED conference, 29-30 September, Levy Institute. http://cooperative-individualism.org/vickrey-william_propositions-relating-to-site-value-taxation-1995.htm
19. T. Nicolaus Tideman (1999), Land Value Taxation is Better than Neutral: Land Taxes, Land Speculation, and the Timing of Development, in Kenneth C. Wenzer (ed.), *Land Value Taxation: The Equitable and Efficient Source of Public Finance*. Armonk, NY: M.E. Sharpe.

Around the world, social activists worked tirelessly to engage with policy-makers and think tanks, and to conduct education programmes for adult students. I had the honour of working alongside all of these people, and more, who flew the flag of ethical economics.

The puzzle is this. These activities were not conducted in secret. Anthony Werner, through his London publishing house (Shepheard-Walwyn) developed a catalogue of books on land and fiscal reform. Yet, according to Brett Christophers, the 40 years since Thatcher was barren on the topic of land.

The conspiracy to divert academia from the economics associated with Henry George is alive and kicking!

Understanding the commons

Rehabilitation of the social sciences requires full disclosure. The stakes could not be higher. The climate crisis illustrates the existential issues. The failure to focus on Rent distorts assessments of how people's relationships with their natural habitats are misaligned. Brett Christophers' omission of the work by Robert V. Andelson (1931-2003), a professor of moral philosophy at Auburn University, Alabama, dramatises the distortions in the prism through which academics view the world.

An article in the journal *Science*, published in 1968, made Garrett Hardin (1915-2003) famous. His thesis, known as *The Tragedy of the Commons*, applied a distorted treatment of the commons to his views on demography and public policy. He argued: "Freedom in a commons brings ruin to all". The ideological implications were clear. *The doctrine authorised the privatisation of land.* Hardin claimed to base his thesis on historical reality: the commons on which people grazed their cattle were unmanaged, and therefore vulnerable to over-exploitation by reckless individuals. This was a false account of the commons, which were not unmanaged.

Nevertheless, Hardin's thesis became a mantra in scholarly articles and books to support theories that favoured land privatisation and/or post-classical economics. Brett Christophers is among the academics in this tradition.[20]

In 1990, Robert Andelson approached Hardin, who was a Professor of Human Ecology in California. The result was a chapter written by Hardin in *Commons Without Tragedy*. Hardin revised his thesis. It was now "The tragedy of the *'Unmanaged'* commons".[21]

There is a world of difference between a managed, and an unmanaged, commons. The doctrine of unmanaged commons favoured the prejudices of the culture of cheating: it biased attitudes and public policy in favour of private land ownership and the privatisation of Rent.

If scholars and their doctoral students had modified their models to take account of Hardin's revised language, new space would have opened up for research into what Andelson called "Commons Without Tragedy: the congruence of Garrett Hardin and Henry George" (the title of Andelson's chapter in *Commons Without Tragedy*).

An account of the commons that was compatible with the fiscal model highlighted by Henry George would have opened up a rich field of academic research. This was not to be. Academia was programmed to treat George as *persona non grata*.

Towards enlightenment

Scientists are human, notes Paul Bloom, Yale professor of psychology and cognitive science, "so we are prone to corruption and groupthink and all sorts of forces that veer us away from

---

20. *The New Enclosure*, op. cit., pp.138-139.
21. Garrett Hardin (1991), "The tragedy of the 'Unmanaged' commons – population and the disguises of providence", in R. V. Andelson (ed), *Commons Without Tragedy*, London: Shepheard-Walwyn. Emphasis added.

Box 5.2 **"The shitty rent business"**

Henry George's *Progress and Poverty* (1879) launched the Rent-based fiscal reform into the centre of public debate. Karl Marx reacted by smearing George as "the capitalist's last ditch".* He characterised "the shitty rent business" as a swindle.**

If Europe had adopted George's fiscal reform in the 19th century, might we have avoided two world wars and the environmental, economic and demographic crises of the 21st century?

* John Haynes Holmes (1947), "Henry George and Karl Marx", *Am J of Econ and Sociology*, p.159.
** Karl Marx and Friedrich Engels (1985), *Collected Works*, 41: 1860-1864. London: Lawrence & Wishart, p.380. Quoted in C. Ward and M.B. Aalbers (2016), "'The shitty rent business': What's the point of land rent theory?" *Urban Studies* 53.

---

the truth".[22] Ben Goldacre, a doctor in Britain's NHS, notes that academics are "as guilty as the rest when it comes to overdramatising their research".[23] Playing fast and loose with the facts of economics, however, is particularly egregious. The damage is transmitted through generations.

That damage is visible in national income statistics, which ought to come with a Health Warning. Governments persist with the Gross Domestic Product metric. In the UK, GDP includes the "value" added by illegal drug trades (about £4bn), while blanking out the value added by charities (reportedly worth £42bn to national income[24]). If economists published shadow national accounts, lawmakers would be embarrassed into amending their practises. That, however, would necessitate a revision to the basic categories of income. Rent, the nation's net income (as distinct

---

22. Paul Bloom (2016), *Against Empathy*, London: Vintage, p.54.
23. Ben Goldacre (2009), *Bad Science*, London: Fourth Estate, p.258.
24. Lord Gus O'Donnell (2021), "National accounts should put a proper value on civil society", Letter, *Financial Times*, Aug. 25.

from commercial rent), would have to be treated as a seprate category. That is a step too far for academics dependent on research grants and tenure in their universities.

Again, to be fair, academics are not solely responsible for arousing delusions about the workings of the economy. Karl Marx promoted his ideology by contributing significantly to the distortion of the social sciences (Box 5.2).

Nevertheless, academics are supposed to honour the rules of objectivity. Failure to comply with that standard comes with heavy risks. In relation to climate warming, for example, Keynyn Brysse and her colleagues scrutinised the predictions of climate scientists and concluded that, in response to peer pressures (such as the accusation of being "alarmist"), they tended to be too cautious in their projections. They gave the syndrome a name: ESLD – erring on the side of least drama.[25] Jargon is one technique for withholding the truth from the public. Prince Charles, a life-long campaigner on behalf of nature, pointedly criticised the use of technical terminology by scientists. He noted that "much of the language being used to describe the situation and the potential remedies is so obscure, sometimes appearing as if it has been chosen to hide the real message and alienate those who most need to hear it."[26]

Scholars need to confront the reality: the manipulation of higher education accommodates doctrinal prejudices. Insidious cases include the project initiated by James Buchanan (1919–2013), who concluded his career at George Mason University in Virginia. His Nobel Memorial Prize was awarded for an economic orientation called "public choice" theory. This rationalised the brand of politics that enshrined "liberty for the wealthy minority above all else and enshrine[d] it in the nation's governing rules".[27]

25. Keynyn Brysse et al (2013), "Climate Change Prediction: Erring on the Side of Least Drama?", *Global Environmental Change* 23(1).
26. www.telegraph.co.uk/news/2021/02/06/prince-charles-ditch-jargon-save-planet/
27. Nancy MacLean (2017), *Democracy in Chains*, New York: Viking Press.

Box 5.3 **"Social silence" on boom/busts**

Mainstream journalism ought to be a source of informed information to guide public debate, but it is subject to what French philosopher Pierre Bourdieu calls "social silence". *Financial Times* journalist Gillian Tett borrowed from the concept to explain how journalists had failed to alert the public to the emerging 2008 financial crisis.

"The media, collectively, should hang its head in shame," she wrote after the event. But when she tried to flag up the dangers, she was challenged both by an absence of relevant information and harassment from bankers who were cashing-in on the sub-prime mortgages that were channelling the financial system towards collapse. In a sincere *mea culpa*, Tett wrote:

> Notwithstanding all that, I could have and should have rung alarm bells more loudly. So could have and should have the rest of the media. A situation in which most business journalists missed the biggest story for decades is not a good situation. I feel strongly that journalists need to recognize that collectively, or we too will lack credibility.*

The media remains constrained to this day, as evidenced by silence on the 2026 economic crash. As ever, there are honourable exceptions.**

* https://slate.com/news-and-politics/2009/03/the-press-and-social-silence.html Bourdieu's account of how the cultural "elite" control the public discourse, is reviewed in Tett's Fool's Gold (2010), New York: Free Press.
** www.thisismoney.co.uk/money/mortgageshome/article-9601221/The-18-year-property-cycle-tips-house-price-boom-crash-2026.html

---

Remedial action is needed because, as economist Steve Keen acknowledges, the next financial crisis is unavoidable. That crisis is coming "because mainstream economists have clung to delusional ideas about the nature of capitalism, even as the real world, time and again, has proven them wrong".[28] Fortunately, some

---

28. Steve Keen (2017), *Can we avoid another financial crisis?* Cambridge: Polity Press, p.129.

academics are seeking to inject human realities back into economics.[29]

Informed debate is the cathartic route to a new constitutional settlement. Who could serve as honest arbitrators on the facts in our post-truth age? Journalists ought to be a source of vital information; too often, they fail (box 5.3). Scholars alone are also unable to fulfil their obligations, in the view of Jo Guldi, an American historian at Southern Methodist University. Her specialist field is the British Empire and the use and ownership of property under capitalism. Aware of the vitality of civil society organisations searching for solutions, she proposes that scholars should team up with citizens to create a "citizen science".[30] Such a collaboration would inspire new ways to recover from the Covid-19 pandemic, if academic reckoning with reality included appreciation of the social role of Rent.

29. Deidre Nansen McCloskey (2021), *Bettering Humanomics: A New, and Old, Approach to Economic Science*, Chicago: Chicago University Press.
30. Jo Guldi (2018), "Global Questions About Rent and the *Longue Durée* of Urban Power, 1848 to the Present", *New Global Studies*, 12(1), p.62.

2024 Countdown

Confessions are rare. Cherish this by a US Federal Reserve economist: "Mainstream economics is replete with ideas that 'everyone knows' to be true, but that are actually arrant nonsense". His three examples lacked "any sort of empirical foundation; moreover, each one turns out to be seriously deficient on theoretical grounds. Nevertheless, economists continue to rely on these and similar ideas to organize their thinking about real-world economic phenomena." [31] *When confronted with Rent-based real-world economics, economists assert: "an effective tax on economic rent would finance only a tiny portion of government expenditures".* [32] *Arrant nonsense!*

31. Jeremy B. Rudd (2021), Why Do We Think That Inflation Expectations Matter for Inflation? (And Should We?), Washington, DC: Federal Reserve Board.
32. Richard Lipsey (1979), *Positive Economics*, 5th edn., London: Weidenfeld & Nicolson, p.371.

CHAPTER SIX

2025 Indictment

When free riding mutates from a personality flaw into a culture which permeates other people's lives, the enablers of rent seeking commit the ultimate crime against humanity.

In its privatised form, and given sufficient time, Rent replicates the pathologies from the original land grabs into an intergenerational power that destroys civilisation. That happened in antiquity. One day, because of colonialism, the perversion of net income would threaten the viability of our species.

That time has come.

To sustain their behaviour, the earliest free riders had to fortify themselves with the trappings of a class-based culture. They had to occupy other people's cultural space. They achieved this by polluting moral values and social practices. Their victims, The Dispossessed, were converted into hostages. The rent seekers eroded society's resilience by consuming the vitality out of communities.

Success came at a price. In time, rent seeking reaches a cannibalistic stage as its insatiable appetite devours the basis of its existence.

In the past, the collapse of civilisations was not fatal to humanity. Communities flourished elsewhere on Earth, where they experimented and evolved new civilisations. That escape route no longer exists. This time, *there is nowhere to hide*. No free spaces on Earth offering refuge from the most lethal social virus on the planet. The Social Galaxy has capitulated to the culture of cheating.

Humanity, instead of resting on rock-solid pillars, hangs on a corrupted thread. There is one way, only, in which to rebuild vitality and renew the evolutionary project. Restore the social status of Rent. Not by placing guilty heads on guillotine blocks. Rather, by open conversations that lead to the consent needed to reform the financial system. Not by shattering cultures, but by honouring the diversity made possible by the evolutionary blueprint.

The first step towards an informed consensus is honest appraisal of the behaviour that has brought humanity to this precipice. To initiate a cathartic conversation, we need a testable proposition.

The culture of Rent privatisation is a crime against humanity.

It

1. *kills people, systematically: taxing them to death by a thousand cuts*

2. *levels down communities, purposefully: depleting their vitality, and*

3. *renders governance irresponsible: dishonouring the duty of care*

The charge of "crime against humanity" appeared in draft form at the 71st session of the UN International Law Commission in 2019.[1] Controversy continues over how such a crime might be enforced (Box 6.1).

---

1. Draft of Articles on Prevention and Punishment of Crimes against Humanity. https://legal.un.org/ilc/texts/instruments/english/draft_articles/7_7_2019.pdf

---

Box 6.1 **Prosecuting the Crime**

In October 2021, the UN's Sixth Committee (Legal) considered whether to establish an international convention on crimes against humanity. Its definition repeated the terms in Article 7 on Crimes against Humanity, in the Rome Statute of the International Criminal Court (ICC).

Opinions of Sixth Committee members differed on whether prosecutions should be under an international convention or by individual States.

Commentators acknowledge that the crime against humanity is more extensive than genocide or war crimes, because it may be committed in situations that do not involve armed conflict or intent to destroy certain groups of people.

There are problems with assigning prosecutorial power to States. Can a State, if it perpetrated the crime, be expected to prosecute itself? Can those who are authorised to define the scope of the crime, under national law, be trusted to include all aspects of the crime?

Contested is the essence of the crime. The word "humanity" is treated as ambiguous, referring either to "humankind" (the species), or the values of humanness. The historical use of the concept indicates preference for the focus on values. That poses a difficulty. In the past, values attributed to humanness co-existed with, accommodated (for example), slavery. The evolutionary blueprint, based on the nomothetic approach to scientific research, settles the issue by identifying the essence of what it took to become human (Box 6.2).

If this knowledge had guided statecraft in the decades since World War 2, we might have avoided the genocides in Yugoslavia, Rwanda and Cambodia. Member nation-states of the UN, however, intentionally decided to limit the definition of genocide. They excluded culture (Box 6.3).

Box 6.2 **The non-negotiable clause**

Nomothetic social science deals with universal statements or laws, and employs quantitative data to explain causal relationships. This provides a broad appreciation and deep understanding of what it means to be human, and of the terms on which humanity evolved.

In Book 1 of *#WeAreRent*, I explained that hominids gravitated out of nature when, at some point in time, that has yet to be determined, they became self-conscious of the benefits from working together to produce resources beyond their daily personal needs. They could invest those resources, the net income, in their bodies and communities. This work ethic deepened their self-awareness, and resulted in greater control over their social prospects and natural habitats.

This meant, however, that early humans committed future generations to a non-negotiable clause in the social contract. For the common good, Rent had to be invested in the legacy assets transmitted to future generations in as good, if not better, state than when they were inherited. Diverting Rent into private uses betrayed the evolutionary project.

Box 6.3 **Cultural genocide**

The atrocities of World War 2 obliged the community of nations to formulate the terms of a crime called genocide.

Raphael Lemkin (1900-1959), a Polish lawyer, coined the concept. He proposed that the crime should include behaviour that caused "disintegration of the political and social institutions, of culture, language, national feelings, religion, and the economic existence of national groups, and the destruction of the personal security, liberty, health, dignity and even the lives of the individuals belonging to such groups".

Lemkin submitted that cultural genocide should feature in the UN Convention on Genocide, as it was "the most important part of the Convention". The provision was deleted. Lemkin was crestfallen. He understood that "the destruction of the cultural pattern of a group" undermined the essence of humanity.*

* Fred Harrison (2012), *The Traumatised Society*, London: Shepheard-Walwyn, pp. vii-ix

The UN continues to avoid a comprehensive definition of crimes against humanity. Its Draft of Articles on Prevention and Punishment of Crimes against Humanity excludes the destruction of the assets on which people rely for their humanity. Crimes perpetrated by the Tax State, as authorised by the "rule of law", are exempt from censure.

Article 2 codifies the crime under 11 headings. The language favours the nexus of values and behaviour that legitimise the property rights and fiscal policies which systematically erode the essence of humanity. Pure coincidence?

The categories include –

► "Murder". Excluded are the deaths wilfully caused by taxes that constrain the freedom to work and sustain life

► "Deportation". Excluded is the exodus of people driven out of the communities of their birth by the cost of housing

► "Apartheid". Excluded is the segregation of low-income families in locations that germinate deprivation and death

On a global scale, nation-states purposefully employ fiscal policies that systematically debase humanity; to the point where humanity is no longer able to sustain itself because of the depletion of its legacy assets.

The power of privately owned Rent-yielding assets now eclipses the reproductive power of the working population. People can no longer add sufficient net resources to fulfil their common needs. This outcome is solely because of the privatisation of Rent, beginning five centuries ago.

► In its social form, Rent fructifies upwards in an ever-widening virtuous circle of growth.

► In its privatised form, Rent implodes at ever-accelerating speeds into a vortex of death and despair.

Does the evidence sustain the charge that democratically elected representatives of the people administer a form of politics that constitutes a crime against humanity?

The evidence must be interrogated across three dimensions: time, space and cultural depth. Can we trace an unbroken chain of causation across a 500-year political and legal landscape?

To render this exercise manageable, I shall focus on the culpability of Westminster, which celebrates its status as the "Mother of Parliaments". The significance of Westminster is evident: Parliament sanctioned the behaviour that turned England, and then the UK, into the leading Coloniser. Portugal and Spain did launch the earliest voyages of plunder across the ocean to South America. England, however, challenged them to become the leading architect of the globalised culture of cheating. Parliament authorised the laws and practices that planted rent seeking in every corner of the globe, until the USA took over as the leading Facilitator of the social virus in the 20th century.

Time: inter-generational inequality

Institutionalised poverty and inequality spans centuries. It embraces families whose ancestors were victims of the original land grabs, the human impact of which was mandated by the laws and fiscal policies evolved by Parliament. The Dispossessed became an inter-generational class of people who were dependant on charity.

Geographer Paul Longley and his colleagues at University College, London, documented the transmission of deprivation across England and Scotland with data that "allows us to chart the different social mobility outcomes experienced by every one of the

13,378 long-established family groups". The family name-based method provides an analytical framework that stretches back to the 12th century. Using family names, charts were developed to depict the fate of people over the course of the last 165 years.

Out-migration from home communities was not the result of a footloose disposition, a lust to wander. People displaced by poverty remained in the state of deprivation when they relocated elsewhere in the UK. The research demonstrated that "there has been no level playing field for any recent generation".

> In defining our population of interest as 'long-settled family groups', we bring focus to the intergenerational inequalities that the British state has bestowed and sustains today.[2]

This conclusion is a clear indictment of the Welfare State, which spans three generations. Seventy years of state-sponsored/tax-funded interventions have not erased the poverty and deprivation that denotes the unequal treatment of citizens under the rule of law.

In condemning the British state's role in the transmission of deprivation through time, I do not deny that some people were, and are, personally responsible for their plight. In the overwhelming majority of cases, however, the pathologies embedded in the social *milieu* deprive people of full control over their lives. People do not choose deprivation as a lifestyle; nor do they intentionally transmit that state to their children and, through them, onwards to generations that span centuries. Social pathologies were germinated by the economics of spatial inequality. The dynamics of spatial inequality are rooted in the rupture of people from the commons. Those ruptures created the traumas that Parliament sustained over the centuries with its fiscal barriers to equality and prosperity.

---

2. Paul A. Longley *et al* (2021), "The geography of intergenerational social mobility in Britain", *Nature Communications*, p.6.

The documented crimes appear in the pages of history books and in news reports in the media of yesteryear and today.

▶ *No right to remain.* The nobility's trump card was the ultimatum to their hostages: *pay Rent, or move on!* The Dispossessed had no choice: deprived of their right to remain in the communities of their birth, to survive, they moved on.

– Colonial Ireland suffered rack-renting imposed by English aristocrats. This provoked mass exodus.[3] Many settled in lowland Scotland, triggering what Longley and his colleagues called "the enduring dearth of opportunities bequeathed upon the descendants of migrants from Ireland".

– Enclosure of commons and clan lands drove the inhabitants of ancient villages into towns. In England, the result was a poor north/rich south divide. In Scotland, the north fares best compared to the southern lowlands according to the UK government's Index of Multiple Deprivation.

– Displacement continues in the 21st century, most visibly by courtesy of the residential property market. House prices force young people to quit home communities in search of affordable shelter.

Displacement, which denotes the loss of the right to remain in home communities, began in the 16th century and continued through to the present time. It cramped people into smaller living spaces in densely inhabited neighbourhoods in large towns. By this method, in the Welfare State, people paid Rent and taxes and survived at the margins with the aid of tax-funded handouts.

---

3. Book 1, *#WeAreRent*, pp. 69-71.

State intervention did not make deprivation disappear. It further embedded poverty as an endemic feature of Parliamentary politics. Today, unable to survive on state subsidies, many families rely on gifts from food banks.[4] One study found that "76% of the food insecure adults in our sample reported being employed".[5]

The Covid pandemic added a further twist to the displacement process. Richly endowed asset owners moved from big towns to rural refuges, which accelerated the rise in rural house prices. Not only did this drive young people from their home communities; it attacked the family unit, "a crucible for anxiety, dysfunction and despair".[6] In 2021, 72% of young people in rural areas said that affordable housing was their top concern; with 84% of those who wanted to leave, saying the cost of shelter was an important factor influencing their decision.[7]

> ▶ *Deaths by a thousand cuts.* Politically induced death is an institutionalised feature of the Tax State.

In the early history of displacement, people were vilified as responsible for their plight. They were called vagrants. Punishments for trekking the by-ways of England included whippings at the stocks, and death.

Economic recessions were particularly painful episodes for those who relied on charity. An egregious example is the long distance land speculation project known as the South Sea bubble. Hard times fell across the kingdom in 1720. People were hungry.

---

4. In Washington, DC, President Biden celebrated Thanksgiving in his first year of office by cooking in a food bank. Darlene Superville (2021), "Biden and Harris help food kitchen prepare Thanksgiving meals ahead of president's Nantucket trip", *Boston Globe*, Nov. 23.

5. Amy Yau *et al* (2020), Socio-demographic characteristics, diet and health among food insecure UK adults, *Public Health Nutrition*, 23(14), p.2612.

6. Tanya Gold (2021), "The lights are going out over Cornwall as locals are driven from their homes", *Daily Telegraph*, Nov. 17.

7. YouGov survey for CPRE (2021), Outpriced and overlooked: Survey on why young people feel forced to leave rural areas, p.3.

To survive, some of them hunted game on what were traditionally the commons. Landlords fought back. Robert Walpole became the first Prime Minister in 1721. He enacted the Black Act (1723), which branded poachers as "wicked and evil". The death penalty awaited those who hunted and ate wild game. Hundreds were hung on the gallows. In the assessment of one author, "no other single statute passed during the 18th century equalled [the Black Act] in severity, and none appointed the punishment of death in so many cases".[8]

In 1965, Parliament abolished capital punishment. Instead, tax-funded attempts to combat problems like poverty amplified the social pathologies. The creation of an Office for Health Improvement and Disparities in 2021 was accompanied by "the starkest evidence yet of the large, persistent and widening inequalities in life expectancy at birth in England. The divide takes many forms – north-south, rich-poor, male-female, London versus the rest of the country".[9]

► 21st century variations in life chances result from variations in the distribution of Rent. Babies born in Drumchapel, a suburb of Glasgow, and in neighbour-hoods of Stockton-on-Tees, in the northeast of England, die a dirty dozen years earlier than their peers in Chelsea, London.

Are politicians culpable? Boris Johnson, as Prime Minister, acknowledged his awareness of the problem. He said so in a speech to his party faithful. He did not accept responsibility for tens of thousands of people who die prematurely every year because of pathologies traceable to the tax-and-tenure paradigm.

8. L. Radzinowicz (1945), "The Waltham Black Act: A study of the legislative attitude towards crime in the eighteenth century", *Cambridge Law Journal*, 9(1).
9. www.kingsfund.org.uk/blog/2021/10/rising-health-inequalities-office-health-im-provement-disparities

Instead, he joked. It worked. He diverted attention from political realities. Referring to the "aching gaps within the regions", he asked:

> What monkey glands are they applying in Ribble Valley...that they live seven years longer than the people of Blackpool only 33 miles away?

The seaside town of Blackpool harbours some of the most deprived communities in Britain. The difference in the life spans between those people, and the residents of rural communities in the Ribble Valley, is not due to anything resembling monkey glands. To distract from the grotesque reality, Johnson resorted to a joke. The inference: the folk in Blackpool did not die prematurely; Ribble Valley residents had access to a secret elixir that extended their lives. The party faithful laughed.[10]

And so, back to Beveridge and "kick it into the long grass" strategy. The Children's Commissioner for England, Dame Rachel de Souza, announced a "Beveridge for Children" project. Children would be asked about their plight. The result, she promised, would be a report that identified "barriers preventing children from reaching their full potential, propose policy and services solutions and develop targets by which improvements can be monitored".[11]

Through the ages, many elected representatives did care for their constituents, but the revenue system prevented them from erasing pathologies such as involuntary unemployment, mental ill-health and the deprivation visible in communities across the land.

---

10. The UK government acknowledges "the wider determinants of health" – social, economic and environmental – which influence mental and physical health. They result in social inequality, "an important driver of...health inequalities". The quality of air, green spaces and housing also affect health. And yet, in its catalogue of determinants, no mention is made of the deadweight impact of fiscal policy on the health of the population. www.gov.uk/government/publications/health-profile-for-england/chapter-6-social-determinants-of-health
For the impact on health in Blackpool, see Life Expectancy (blackpooljsna.org.uk)
11. https://www.childrenscommissioner.gov.uk/report/the-childhood-commission/

Space: the global plunder

Statistics reveal the overwhelming influence of the rent seeking culture across the planet. Researchers at McKinsey Global Institute crunched the numbers for the 10 countries that generate more than 60% of global income.[12] The numbers understate the statistical significance of Rent. Nevertheless, the findings leave no doubt that our world is hostage to the culture of cheating.

▶ Real assets and net worth in 2020 reached $500 trillion. Two-thirds were in the form of real estate, "raising questions about whether societies store their wealth productively". Of the gains in real estate, "some 55% derived from higher land prices".

▶ Residential real estate amounted to almost half of global net worth. Corporate and government real estate accounted for an additional 20%. The most significant driver of growth of household real estate stock "was rising land prices, accounting for more than half of the increased value of global household real estate".[13]

▶ McKinsey hinted that the global economy had reached its zenith, alluding to "a new paradigm of persistently high asset prices". The possibility that governance, through the choice of fiscal policies, played a leading role in the runaway price trends in property markets, was not explored.

---

12. Australia, Canada, China, France, Germany, Japan, Mexico, Sweden, the UK and USA.
13. Jonathan Woetzel *et al* (2021), The rise and rise of the global balance sheet: How productively are we using our wealth? New York: McKinsey Global Institute, pp. vi, 18, 80, 144.

The "new paradigm" arrived via multiple routes. The free riding virus, by deploying its corrupting variations, supplanted culturally diverse social systems.

► *The commercial variant* in China: the attempt to build a non-capitalist society of equals defeated by workers who assembled property portfolios. This created an ideological crisis. President Xi branded real estate as Enemy No 1 in 2021 as he struggled to equalise life chances.

► *The corporate variant* in Africa: natural resources traded on terms that create failed states like the Democratic Republic of Congo. People occupying the inner circles of power bribed by western entrepreneurs, with racketeering at the expense of the public purse and people's welfare.

► *The criminal variant* in South America: autocrats, desperate to remain in power, tolerate drug-trading gangs that duel to control resource rents. Costs of political corruption are displaced onto nature's habitats, indigenous peoples and the opioid consumers of North America.

The historic link between net worth and GDP disappeared at the beginning of the 21st century.

Cultural depth

To sustain the charge of a crime against humanity, we need the statistics of a Whole-of-Life Budget. This would reveal how societies are haemorrhaging wealth in all of its forms – not just material, but also psychological, spiritual and social wealth. Governments avoid full disclosure. The Whole-of-Life Budget would provoke people into holding their political representatives to account. We can offer, however, a portrait of the cultural depth of the corruption embedded in the fabric of society resulting from the withdrawal of Rent from the common good.

The Social Galaxy reached the inflexion point and entered the cannibalistic age in the 1980s. Humanity was on the road to dystopia. To prove guilt, however, we need to demonstrate an unbroken fiscal/financial chain of causation across five centuries in The Making of the Tax State.

In the beginning, the struggle for power was between absolute monarchs and their wayward feudal barons. Knights and barons aspired to independence from medieval monarchs, from whom they held land on condition that they rendered services to the nation. Economic independence, however, could only come by working for their living (thereby adding value to the wealth of the nation). The alternative: become free riders.

1. *The power grab.* Power gravitated from kings to noblemen (16th to 17th centuries). Parliament was the site of contest. Laws enacted to privilege the nobility. Their lordships retained decision-making power by imposing a landed property qualification on the right to vote.

2. *Irresponsible governance.* Fiscal legislation (18th to 19th centuries) shifted government revenue away from Rent and onto the wages of labour and the profits of capital. Class-based politics and fiscal policies generated pathologies for which the landlords were not held accountable.

3. *Hereditary rights.* Attempts in the 20th century to eliminate the hereditary right to sit in the House of Lords were defeated. Noblemen clung on to their seats! Lord David Trefgarne, in 2021 the longest serving peer: "Don't tell me we know nothing about democracy. We invented it!"[14]

---

14. George Parker (2021), "Born this way", *FT Weekend Magazine*, Nov. 13, p.23.

It took 500 years, but aristocrats from the era that historians call "bastard feudalism" triumphed. Their scions diminished, and then erased from the fabric of society, the evolutionary paradigm that sustained institutional harmony, communal resilience and social justice. In its place, they planted in people's minds the cornerstones of the paradigm that accommodated their insatiable appetites.

At this point, defence lawyers would introduce their clinching objection. Under universal suffrage, people had the power to overrule predatory behaviour in favour of equality before the law.

Over the course of the 20th century, vigorous attempts were made to reform the Westminster model of finance.

They failed.

The guilty mind

To prove that rent privatisation is a crime against humanity, we have to reveal a "guilty mind": a conscious intention to continue with behaviour that results in outcomes repugnant to norms of justice.

In the case of the culture of cheating, free riding had to persist across five centuries. To do so, the guardians of that culture had to employ antennae that were sensitive to threats against the private appropriation of Rent. When the alarm bells rang, purposeful action had to defuse the threats. The greatest threat did come with universal suffrage in the 20th century. Three attempts were made to counter free riding.

1. *The first attempt.* 1909-1920: a Liberal government began to rebase revenue on Rent. The House of Lords successfully challenged the Commons.

Not content with abolishing the reform, which was instituted by the People's Budget (1910), their lordships demanded reimbursement of the Rent they had begun to pay into the public purse. Parliament obliged in 1920.

> 2. *The second attempt.* 1931-1934: a Labour Chancellor introduced the Rent-as-public-revenue policy. This time, opposition came from within the Commons.

Philip Snowden, the Chancellor of the Exchequer, was disgusted. Politicians of all parties resisted his fiscal reform. He denounced the hypocrisy and lies from Liberal, Labour and Conservative politicians who wanted exemptions for their land.[15]

> 3. *The third attempt.* 1945-1980: Labour governments sought to reform the land market and draw revenue from Rent; a strategy buried by Margaret Thatcher.

From then on, free riding faced no serious opposition. Marx's industrial proletariat capitulated, the *coup de grâce* executed when Thatcher converted the working class into shock troops for the culture of cheating. She sold public housing to council tenants at knockdown prices. Her "property owning democracy" doctrine was a smokescreen. Owners of the most valuable locations (such as the aristocrats who occupied extensive estates in the heart of London) and those who owned Rent-yielding assets (such as financiers) were free to ride on the backs of tax-paying wage earners.

This history emphasises the role of the Executive. What of the administration, the civil servants who advise politicians? They, too, are acutely sensitive to the need not to tamper with the value of land, if we believe the man who once served as HM Treasury's top economist. Nick Macpherson was even elevated, as Permanent Secretary, to the top post in the Treasury. He occasionally dared to wonder whether the UK would be better off with a fiscal charge on Rent.

---

15. Philip Snowden (1934), *An Autobiography*, Vol.2, London: Ivor Nicholson and Watson, pp.905-921

> It worries me...that we don't have a land tax. In a sane world, we would have a proper land tax. Sadly the only person to try it was Lloyd George and he ended up having to pay every single penny back.[16]

Macpherson revealed the psychic depth of the prejudice against any discussion on that subject. He was dismissed as "insane" when he raised the prospect of shifting the revenue base on to Rent.[17]

Logical incompetence

The tax tools favoured by lawmakers ensure that revenue always falls short of the sums needed to fund the welfare services that people require. There is a logic to this incompetence. The only proportionate relationship between public income, and people's needs, is the one offered by Rent-as-public-revenue. That policy is disallowed under the Westminster model of governance. The outcome is an apparently shambolic administration of law making and enforcement. There are two ways to view this state of affairs. One is that the model of governance is flawed; the other is that, on the contrary, it is successful by design.

The first view was voiced in a blistering critique of UK governance offered by Kate Bingham, who chaired the UK's Vaccine Taskforce in 2020. In a lecture at Oxford University, she drew on her exposure to the way Whitehall and Westminster operated, noting "a devastating lack of skills and experience in science, industry, commerce and manufacturing". Ignorance was compounded by "the lack of commercial and scientific skills among the Cabinet as well as Whitehall, which too often led to a lack of trust born of ignorance, and a routine assumption among officials that businesses have no motive beyond greed". Dame Bingham offered no hope for improvement.

---

16. Lord Macpherson, statement, Resolution Foundation seminar, October 24, 2018.
17. Macpherson's "insane" statement can be viewed here: tps://www.resolutionfoundation.org/events/ light-at-the-end-of-the-tunnel-will-it-be-anend-of-austerity-budget/

> More deeply, government seems to have no means, and little interest, to detect the differences between negative rent-seeking and economically valuable corporate behaviour.[18]

She lamented government's lack of "interest to detect the differences between money-grabbing opportunism and valuable corporate behaviour". Instead of deploying the requisite skills for a problem-solving form of governance, Whitehall and Westminster were replete with "historians and economists, few of whom, it seems, have ever worked outside Whitehall".

Dame Bingham attributed the incompetence to a flaw in the Westminster model. The alternative interpretation is that UK governance is eminently successful, performing exactly as designed by its rent seeking architects. Skills that pointed to solutions would embarrass the guardians of the culture of cheating. Policy proposals that limited the freedom to transfer Rent from value-adders to free riders – which would solve problems – could not be countenanced!

Stocking Westminster and Whitehall with historians and economists – generalists, a disproportionate number of whom gravitated to the centre of power via Eton and Oxford – is culturally programmed into the system. They operate within a philosophical framework designed to maximise Rents.

An almost endless sequence of official and unofficial investigations assessed the performance of governance, which verified institutional incompetence. Tax-funded political institutions betray vulnerable citizens. Is it surprising that people nurture a profound distrust of government? Lord Evans, the former chief of the Secret Service who chairs the independent Committee on Standards in Public Life, echoed the popular view when he declared that Britain could "slip into becoming a corrupt country".[19]

---

18. www.ox.ac.uk/news/2021-11-24-another-war-coming-kate-bingham-dbe-delivers-romanes-lecture
19. www.theguardian.com/politics/2021/nov/04/standards-committee-chair-attacks-tory-dismantling-anti-sleaze-system

▶ *The law makers.* It took a newspaper, the *Daily Telegraph* (in 2009), to name MPs who fiddled their expenses, exposing one version of the "sleaze" that shames Parliament at the expense of taxpayers.[20]

Not all parliamentarians were, or are, self-serving. Nonetheless, the litany of wilful failures – either as members of the Executive, or from the backbenches of Parliament – is long and, in too many cases, mortal. Like the case of the Grenfell Towers disaster, the London skyscraper that claimed 72 lives when it went up in smoke in 2017. In the enquiry that followed the Johnson government admitted that, over the previous two decades, successive governments had engaged in covering up the risks associated with the combustible materials used as cladding on buildings.[21]

▶ *The law enforcers.* Enacting laws that are not enforced is a pointless exercise. Following the 2008 financial crisis, Parliament chose not to rebase its finances on a sustainable footing. Instead, it imposed "austerity".

The savage cuts in public services, following the financial crisis of 2008, included the closure of half of the police stations that were supposed to protect communities.[22] Vulnerable people were left exposed, like victims of rape: women cannot expect justice because of "systemic failings" in the administration of the law, which failed to deal with complaints made by victims "at all stages of the criminal justice process", confessed the Justice Secretary.[23]

The failure of the law to protect children is an inter-generational crime. From paedophile gangs to priests in cloisters, children have

---

20. https://mpsallowances.parliament.uk/mpslordsandoffices/hocallowances/allowances-by-mp/
21. www.theguardian.com/uk-news/2021/dec/07/grenfell-inquiry-government-deeply-sorry-for-past-failures
22. George Odling (2021), "Justice in Retreat", *Daily Mail*, March 1.
23. U.K. Justice System Has Failed Rape Victims, Government Says – The New York Times (nytimes.com)

been sexually abused in towns across the country in a process that is heart breaking to read about in the newspapers. The most recent investigation, into abuse perpetrated within religious institutions, noted that blaming the victims was one of the ways to protect the perpetrators.[1]

► *The law enablers.* The "jewel" in the UK's Welfare State is the National Health Service. For too many expectant mothers, hospitals became mortuaries.

Because of under-funding and poor administration, hundreds of babies have died, or suffered brain damage, in NHS hospitals across the country, from Shrewsbury in the West Midlands to East Kent in the South-east. In the case of Nottingham University Hospitals NHS Trust, patients were told that theirs were one-off tragedies. The evidence did not support this attempt to escape responsibility: bereaved families received more than £91m in damages and legal costs since 2010.[2]

Medical staffs in NHS hospitals are heroes, caring for patients, day-in, day-out. The repetitive nature of the avoidable deaths and damage to mothers and babies, however, is on a scale that reveals institutional failure. The failure, ultimately, must be traced back to funding from government. Too frequently, hospitals are under-staffed and under-trained.

Because of the deadweight burdens imposed by taxation, ill-heath surfaces in so many forms and places. In 2013, the wider costs to the UK economy of mental ill-health were estimated by the Chief Medical Officer at £70-100 billion a year (4.5% of GDP).[3] According to the Confederation of British Industry, 63% of time lost to poor health are in the working age popu-

1. www.iicsa.org.uk/document/child-protection-religious-organisations-and-settings-investigation-report-september-2021
2. www.independent.co.uk/news/health/nottingham-hospitals-maternity-baby-deaths-b1874132.html
3. Mental health statistics: global and nationwide costs | Mental Health Foundation

Box 6.6 **Guilty as charged**

► Consequences arising from laws and revenue policies are intentional.

► Segregation results from class-based privatisation of net income.

► Gesture politics authorise the postcode lottery of premature deaths.

► Governments and their institutions are culpable for their past deeds, and guilty of prolonging the crime against humanity.

lation, with the annual cost in lost output estimated at £300bn (excluding treatment costs).[4] In the rented housing sector, because government fails to enforce the law on Category 1 hazards (defined as serious threats to health and safety), over 580,000 properties fall into that category. According to the National Audit Office, this negligence created "the associated costs to the NHS... estimated to be £340 million a year".[5]

The Verdict

Proof beyond doubt exists that the Westminster model of democratic politics is a crime against humanity. In the court of public opinion, the verdict would be "Guilty!" See Box 6.6.

4. www.cbi.org.uk/seize-the-moment/a-healthier-nation/
5. National Audit Office (2021), Regulation of private renting, p.7. www.nao.org.uk/wp-content/uploads/2021/09/Regulation-of-private-renting.pdf

Figure 6.1 **The Fiscal Pincer**

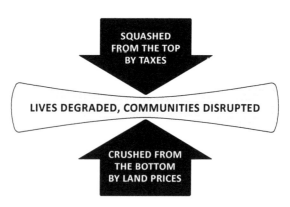

Nation-states wilfully employ the fiscal system that privileges free riders, wilfully impose painful pathologies on The Dispossessed, while disclaiming responsibility for the consequences. The crime is committed by squeezing people in a pincer movement (Fig.6.1).

Not discussed in political circles, but not a secret to dissenting economists, is the root cause. Joseph Stiglitz insists that inequality is not an intrinsic feature of market economics. He attributes inequality to "the growth in rents — including land and exploitation rents (e.g., arising from monopoly power and political influence)". His analysis showed that "the increases are closely related to increases in land prices...largely, related to increases in the value of land. A tax on the return to land, and even more so, on the capital gains from land, would reduce inequality and, by encouraging more investment into real capital, actually enhance growth".

Nor does he begrudge credit where it is due: "This is, of course, an old idea, promoted most famously by Henry George (1879)".[6]

Because governments refuse to neutralise the culture of cheating, the people of a disunited kingdom are reduced to a state of dependency and discrimination. The ONS reports: "51.5% of households received more in benefits (including in-kind benefits such as education) than they paid in taxes in 2013/14. This is equivalent to 13.7 million households".[7] Reform activists characterise Welfare State interventions as necessary to reduce poverty. In reality, the Welfare State embeds poverty in a deep freeze, by accommodating taxes that amplify the trauma inflicted on working people, trauma rooted in the original land grabs.

From grassroots to the global sphere, we need new ways of living. The only way to permanently enhance the fabric of society is by reforming fiscal policy. Complex societies need authority structures. Governance facilitates the provision of services people cannot provide for themselves. Public agencies cannot function without the flow of resources that match people's needs. To participate in such a system, every citizen needs to contribute to the required resources. The quality of governance and its decision-making is contingent on how revenue is raised.

Restoring humanity to the evolutionary path will require a unified act to shift the *zeitgeist*, the spirit and mood that define our period of history, as revealed by commonly held ideas and beliefs. This entails cathartic conversations that lead to a consensus on the alternative status of property rights and government revenue, and a mandate for reforms that deliver an authentic democracy.

---

6. Joseph E. Stiglitz (2015), "The Origins of Inequality, and Policies to Contain It", *National Tax Journal*, 68(2), pp.442-443. http://dx.doi.org/10.17310/ntj.2015.2.09
7. www.ons.gov.uk/peoplepopulationandcommunity/
personalandhouseholdfinances/incomeandwealth/bulletins/
theeffectsoftaxesandbenefitsonhouseholdincome/2015-06-29

Media editors focus attention on the inefficiencies of economic instability. Yet, these are far eclipsed by the human tragedies that are endured by people, day in, day out, across the land; most of which would be avoided, if their governments were not guilty of the crime against humanity.

2025 Countdown

When Barbados severed its link with the British crown, by declaring itself a republic, Prince Charles, the heir to the throne, acknowledged "the appalling atrocity of slavery". Representing the Queen at the Bridgetown ceremony on Nov. 29, 2021, he declared that the crime against humanity "forever stains our history". This was a bold introduction to a cathartic conversation. Will the peoples of the western democracies follow the prince's lead and "clear the decks", so that they can restore justice to the way they lead and govern their lives?

CHAPTER SEVEN

2026 Cascade

It is the most enormous real-time experiment in the history of social science. Test the hypothesis by tracking housing markets to a peak in 2026, observe the global economy crash into its deepest vortex since the 1930s, and then monitor four existential crises converging on 2030. Everyone in the world suffers.

We know what follows, from former times. Cities in Egypt and along the Euphrates overrun by boatpeople who sailed in from the west. Rome overrun by mass migration from the north. Migrants were not responsible for the fall of those civilisations. They were already imploding from within. Their termination is a story that begins and ends with the displacement of people from their home communities. Migrants were just one of the elements in the four existential crises, in ancient times.

So it is, today, for western civilisation. Governments that refuse to prepare for this catastrophe will be complicit in the ultimate crime against humanity. The cascading warning signs abound. There is one way only to rehabilitate our globalised civilisation: through the cathartic conversations that lead to truth and reconciliation.

Truth is what the culture of cheating cannot tolerate. That is evident in the way economists analyse boom/bust cycles in the housing market. They refuse to highlight the responsibility of privatised Rent. The facts, however, are not ambiguous.

An IMF analysis of systemic banking crises concluded: "more than two thirds were preceded by boom-bust patterns in house prices".[1] House prices are a proxy for land values. More than two-thirds is statistically significant. Yet, that proportion understates the primacy of Rent in causing banking crises.

Some systemic banking crises are not apparently linked to "house" prices. True. Appearances, however, are deceiving, which enables the IMF to place responsibility for the instability on stock markets. Probe deeper, to find out who creates instability in the price of shares traded in the markets.

Investors gravitate towards shares in enterprises that draw much of their "profits" from Rental income. Those shares are attractive, either because they deliver high rewards via capital gains, or because they come at a relatively lower risk than shares in commercial enterprises that make their money by producing goods and services for customers. By pouring money into shares heavily anchored in Rent, a frenzy is sparked which triggers stock market booms that drive prices to unsustainable levels. The target enterprises include construction companies, real estate investment trusts, and IT corporations whose income is almost exclusively the Rent of the electro-magnetic spectrum. As for banks: these add to the fever of speculation by favouring financial transactions where land is the collateral. That biases investments in favour of increasingly high-risk deals. So-called "financialisation" is no more than land speculation once removed.

When stock markets and the banking sector drive Rent above sustainable levels, recessions follow. Thus, the IMF's two-thirds

---

1. Christopher Crowe *et al* (2011), How to Deal with Real Estate Booms: Lessons from Country Experiences", IMF Working Paper, p.5.

Figure 7.1 **UK mortgage debt, house prices and income ratios**

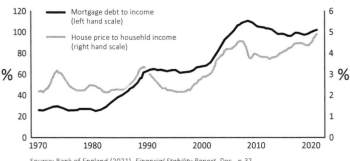

Source: Bank of England (2021), *Financial Stability Report*, Dec., p.32

estimate skilfully understates the causal significance of Rent in unstable markets. We should ignore the IMF's claim that "Bubbles remain hard to spot with certainty".[2] This is wilful blindness. If they looked with open minds, they would spot the bubbles with certainty. There can be no excuse for the international financial institutions to be caught unaware of the 2028 depression.

Figure 7.1 traces the relationship between mortgage debt and house prices in the UK over the three post-war cycles. Mortgages were manageable for post-war baby-boomers. That changed when Margaret Thatcher and Ronald Reagan deregulated the financial sector in the 1980s. The cost of mortgages rose faster than incomes because financiers became active (albeit once removed) land speculators. Sub-prime mortgages were nothing to worry about. Whatever happened, they would not lose. They hold property deeds as collateral for loans. That insulated them against

2. Christopher Crowe *et al* (2011), Policies for Macro-financial Stability: Options to Deal with Real Estate Booms, IMF Research Department, p.5.

the risks of the burden of "house" prices as these increased towards the 1992 crash; and then again up to the 2010 crash. Bankers were never going to pay the price for their recklessness: they were "too big to fail".

Cuckoo in the nest

The genius of the earliest free riders is revealed by the way they learnt to inhabit other people's lives, living in plain sight, without being recognised. Cuckoos in the human nests. The victims know there is something terribly wrong. One symptom: for new home-owners, today, it will take 40 years to pay off the mortgages on their nests.

According to the authorised doctrine of capitalism, everyone has an equal chance. Mellody Hobson, who chairs the Starbucks Corporation and is a director of JP Morgan Chase, a Wall Street investment bank, knows the reality. "US capitalism promises an equal opportunity to compete and succeed. And yet, systemic inequalities exist."[3] Hobson was exceptional. As a child, she was raised in poverty. At one point, her family was homeless. Today, she is a member of *Forbes* magazine's list of the 100 Most Powerful Women in the World. What she has not discovered, however, is the source of systemic inequality. And yet, the evidence continues to stare us in the face.

The most blatant example is provided by the USA, where people continue to believe in the "exceptionalism" of the American model. Donald Trump provided the clearest evidence of rent seeking as the organising mechanism that drives the social system. That model, however, has exhausted itself. We have only to turn to the financial pages of the mainstream media to see the same story played out everywhere in the world. Chile is a classic case

---

3. Mellody Hobson (2021), "The US must confront financial illiteracy head-on", *Financial Times*, Dec. 19.

study of how the cuckoo contorts civil society and the political process to live off the labours of others, in the process triggering social catastrophe.

The South American drama unfolded in two acts, each lasting two decades. First, there was the dictatorship of Gen. Augusto Pinochet in a country that is the world's largest copper producer. Enter economists from the University of Chicago, one of the leading schools for promoting the rent seeking doctrine.[4] They urged Pinochet to privatise natural resources in what we may view as an experiment to test "neo-classical economics". The dictatorship ended in 1990. Now, supervised by the culture of cheating, it was the turn of democracy.

The population engaged in dead-end discourses: jousts between the norms of capitalism and socialism. This lasted for two decades, before the explosion of popular discontent (the *Estallido Social*, or social outburst). In 2019, the people could bear their burdens no longer. Underfunded public services, inadequate pensions and wages that could not cover rents led to the burning of metro stations and churches and looting of shops.

The statistics speak for themselves. Chile is the richest country in South America. With its resource Rents seeping away, however, and with commercial life blighted by corruption, Chile suffered the shame of being the most unequal country in the OECD (Figures 7.2a and 7.2b).

The people demanded a new constitution. The constitutional convention faced an impossible task. Debates took the form of philosophical contests, rather than the open-minded quest for consensus to serve the common good. The ideological conflict culminated in a divisive presidential election between candidates of the extremes – Left and Right (the left-winger won).

---

4. Mason Gaffney (1994), "Neo-classical Economics as a Stratagem against Henry George", in *The Corruption of Economics*, London: Shepheard-Walwyn, p.77.

Figure 7.2a **GDP *per capita***
$ purchasing power parity (2021)

Source: IMF

Figure 7.2b **Income inequality**
is the highest in the OECD (2020)

1 = maximum inequality

Source: IMF

Never the twain shall meet to deliver bottom-up growth towards an inclusivity that rested on peace and prosperity. It could not have been otherwise.

Understanding the organising mechanism that directs these outcomes is vital, if the United States and Europe are to cope with the desperate migrants from the east and south who will arrive in the 2030s.

Policy paralysis

Early indicators of the cascading crises expose one critical feature of the structural vulnerabilities – political paralysis. Western governments agonise over how to stem the tide of illegal migrants who are laying siege to their territorial borders. Instead of firing off pathetic complaints about the migrants, why not ask this question: *what would it take to reinstate the right of those people to remain in their homelands?*

The question is not asked, because it would direct analysis to the one issue that would offend the prevailing – the predatory – culture. So conversations remain riddled with old prejudices, such as the one seeded by Thomas Malthus in the 19th century. Poverty, he argued, was the result of high fertility rates that, in turn, were the result of poverty. The circular argument did not disturb Malthus or those who, today, continue to believe that the world's problems are due to over-population. So the poor were responsible for their plight: they needed to suppress their sexual urges. That reasoning suited the landlords. It distracted attention away from property rights and the tax regime, which deprive people of the right to work and meet their needs in their home communities.

When the 18-year cycle ends in 2028, we can expect western governments to exploit illegal migrants as scapegoats. That blame-game has already started. Politicians use the criminals who direct the flow from Africa and the Near East as their No. 1 targets. Meanwhile, that flow is playing into the hands of autocrats (in countries like Turkey and Belarus) who are destabilising the democracies to distract their own people from the frustrations of their failed systems.

Italy will offer a fascinating case study for historians, who will compare 21st century events with what happened 1,500 years ago. Over the coming years, because of a declining fertility rate, the population will rapidly decline. This will create space for migrants when the torrent begins in 2028. This time, however, there is one major difference. Rome's "barbarians" supplanted the nobility on estates that were scattered around the empire. This time, refugees will occupy the homes vacated by the contracting population. Unless, of course, Europe finds ways to help the migrants to remain in the communities of their birth. To do that, they will need to recommend Whole-of-Life solutions of the kind that deploy the power to avoid existential catastrophes (Box 7.1).

Box 7.1 **Penitence, or what?**

Gambia originated as a fort, the base for slave traders on the west coast of Africa. The Dutch and French fought over its possession, until the English took control in the 17th century. From those harrowing origins sprang the smallest of African countries.

Gambia has a population of under 2.5m people, most of whom are young, very poor, and who endure an unemployment rate of 35%. Government is failing. Instead of investing to develop the country, the fiscal strategy – as prescribed by institutions like the World Bank – sustains the status quo. When the global slump comes, caravans of those young Africans will head north through Morocco and across the narrow straits into Spain.

Gambians need support for a route map back to the evolutionary pathway. Europe owes them that much. There is no point in sending IMF or World Bank economists to the country. Nor is money the solution: no amount would compensate the indigenous peoples whose ancestors had to accommodate the slave traders.

Fiscal reform is the remedy to the world's problems. That harsh reality, however, is excluded from political debates because it raises the one taxing question that democratic politicians are not willing to contemplate.

The taxing question

Instituting a justice-based fiscal system would eliminate the capital value of land beneath people's homes. That is the one issue which now sustains the culture of cheating, and which perpetuates the crime against humanity in its democratic guise.

Homeowners were not willing conspirators in the crime against humanity. They did not consent to the emergence of free riding as a way of life. Through the generations, their ancestors were drilled into the doctrines of rent seeking by the need for homes in which

Figure 7.3 **Who owns England?**
Percentage of land

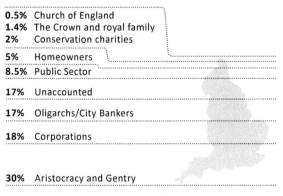

0.5%	Church of England
1.4%	The Crown and royal family
2%	Conservation charities
5%	Homeowners
8.5%	Public Sector
17%	Unaccounted
17%	Oligarchs/City Bankers
18%	Corporations
30%	Aristocracy and Gentry

Source: Guy Shrubsole (2020), *Who Owns England?* London: William Collins, p.267.

to raise their families. The culture they inherited shaped them to the point where, today, few people question the foundations on which their communities are constructed.

The nobility are no longer in numerical control of Parliament. They do not need to be. Their culture successfully hooked the middle class, with the doctrine of "an Englishman's home is his castle". Attitudes and aspirations of homeowners who are "on the property ladder" now guide governments. The spirit of the aristocracy lives on through the residential market.

The aristocracy and nobility own an estimated 30% of the land of England (Figure 7.3).[5] Residential land accounts for 5% of the total: crumbs off the tables of the nobility. Sufficient bait, however, to compromise the working population.

---

5. The nobility also own a substantial part of the land whose owners are not identifiable. The Land Registry declines to use its database to construct an official account of land distribution in England.

Five per cent: a small price to pay for an invincible barrier against reforms to the way governments raise revenue. Five per cent: sufficient to rupture the political will and moral status of the nation. The pathologies created by the original land enclosures continue to pollute people's minds. The badge of honour bestowed on homeowners is a burden of up to 40 years: mortgages are treated as deeds of achievement.

To skew policies in favour of the culture of cheating, governments apply techniques of duplicity. In particular, they disallow "full and fair discussion" on fiscal policy. In particular, statistics that quantify the deadweight losses created by taxes are excluded from budget documents.

The tax tools employed by governments were never authorised by the people of the commons. That puzzled Lysander Spooner (1808–1887), an American anarchist who argued for "no taxation without explicit consent".

> Taxation without consent is as plainly robbery, when enforced against one man, as when enforced against millions... Taking a man's money without his consent, is also as much robbery, when it is done by millions of men, acting in concert, and calling themselves a government, as when it is done by a single individual, acting on his own responsibility, and calling himself a highwayman.

Under the common law of England, Spooner observed, people should consent before being taxed. In the centuries before universal suffrage, the people of the commons were not consulted about whether – or how – they should be taxed. Yet, under the prevailing laws of England it was assumed that people had consented "because some pretended representative, whom he never authorized to act for him, has taken it upon himself to consent that he may be [taxed]". Spooner was brutally frank. The revenue regime rested on "force, fraud, and conspiracy, on the part of kings, nobles, and 'a few wealthy freeholders'".[6]

6. Lysander Spooner (1852), *An Essay on the Trial by Jury*, Cleveland, Ohio: Jewett & Co., p.224.

Homeowners, though now co-opted into the culture of cheating, are not culpable. But that leaves outstanding the issue of what to do about the capital gains from land. The issue of compensation offers no solution.

Compensation for whom, or what?

An authentic democracy would fund public services out of Rent. Landowners would lose a significant part of the value of their assets. They would seek compensation for their loss. But if justice is the guiding principle, we cannot exclude from consideration the rights of others to compensation.

The legal case, under UK law, is set out in the Compensation Act (1961). When a public agency needs privately owned land, landowners are not merely reimbursed for what they originally paid for the land. They can also claim for the value they expected to reap in the future ("hope" value). This means, "the legal rules that govern the land market require the returns from monopoly pricing to flow through to landowners".[7] The outcome: owners are indifferent to whether they keep or lose the land. Compensation is their "ideal solution".

The Office for National Statistics (ONS) has measured the scale of what is at stake. Land, it noted, is a "non-produced asset".

> ▶ 2019: the mid-cycle downturn in the 18-year cycle
> clocked in on time: the value of land declined. Overall,
> however, "In most years the growth in net worth is
> driven by changes to the value of land. Since 1995,
> changes in the value of land have broadly accounted for
> just under two-thirds of the increase in net worth".

---

7. Thomas Aubrey (2018), *Reforming the land market*, London: Centre for Progressive Policy, p.3.

► 2020: alluding to the ATCOR effect: "A rise in the value of land in 2020 increased growth of the household sector's net worth by 3.8 percentage points, and was the result of an 8.1% increase in UK average house prices. The reduction in stamp duty rates are likely to be a main factor driving increases in house prices".

► 2021: land was the largest contributor to growth in household net worth, with net worth growing to £11.2 trillion. Land contributed 40.1% of growth in households' net worth, driven by a 7.3% increase in average house prices. "This rise was likely to have been affected by the reduction in stamp duty rates."[8]

The ONS emphasised that "Land and pension schemes were the largest contributors to growth in households' net worth". By December 2021, net worth had risen to £11.4 trillion. This dwarfed trends in the public sector. The net worth of government assets "fell by £445 billion in 2020, this is the largest fall on record".

The statistics are hard to comprehend. It helps to put a face to an all-too-human problem (Box 7.2).

In considering the issue of compensation, however, we need to consider the legal and moral arguments from the point of view of three models of property rights.

► *The free riding culture.* Compensation is owed for the loss of the future stream of Rents (which determines the capital value of land). In 1833, the doctrine was invoked when Parliament abolished slavery. Slave owners were paid money that the UK government borrowed. The debt remained a burden on taxpayers until 2015. Slaves were not compensated for their losses.

---

8. ONS (2021), National balance sheet estimates for the UK: Statistical bulletin, December 2, p.4.

Box 7.2 **Growing rich while sleeping**

John Stuart Mill, the 19th century philosopher, observed that landowners "grow rich in their sleep without working, risking or economizing. The increase in the value of land, arising as it does from the efforts of an entire community, should belong to the community and not to the individual who might hold title".

TV mogul Simon Cowell bought a London property for £12m. He invested £1m in improvements, so that the Wimbledon dwelling would afford him and his family a spacious home. He then discovered problems with accessing the school of choice for his children, so he put the property up for sale in 2021.

The asking price was £3m above what Cowell paid for the property. If he found a buyer at that price, he would reap a £2m gain after deducting the £1m cost of improvements. Two million pounds, tax-free. What is the moral case for compensating the reality TV entrepreneur for the loss of that £2m, if people democratically decided to restructure the fiscal regime and collect the location value of every property in the UK?

The US government paid reparations to its slave owners: about $300 per enslaved person. For slaves, 40 acres and a mule was offered as compensation. President Andrew Johnson overturned the order and restored the land to former slave-owning planters. The culture of rent seeking survived the civil war.

► *The Clean Slate precedent.* Civilisations in antiquity restored land to the original holders; non-commercial debts were cancelled. This sustained governance by priests and princes. It did not alter the economic practices that, periodically, drove families (in times of drought) to turn to moneylenders for help; offering land as collateral.

During the 50 years between Clean Slate proclamations, losses were inflicted not just on individual families, but also on their cultures and communities. So it has been in modern times under the slave model of land ownership. How do we compensate for those losses? What is the value of the losses inflicted on people who were enslaved in the New World? Thomas Craemer, professor of public policy at the University of Connecticut, has conservatively estimated the cash value at \$14 trillion.[9] Missing from that calculation are the losses to Africa. Across the continent, deprivation was endured at three levels:

► *Human costs:* break-up of extended families, on which people relied to sustain themselves economically and biologically.

► *Cultural costs:* rupture of communities and cultures, on which people relied for guidance through times good and bad.

► *Ecological costs:* displacement forced people to abandon the practices that harmonised their societies with habitats.

These ruptures stalled evolutionary progress. Communities lost the Rents that would have accrued but for the transport of many millions of people to the New World. The slaves did produce Rents. That net income surfaced on the cotton and cane plantations, and was invested in the New World and the European countries that sponsored slave-based agriculture.[10] As a result, poverty blighted Africa.[11]

---

9. https://magazine.uconn.edu/2020/06/15/the-new-reparations-math/#
10. Howard French (2021), *Born in Blackness: Africa, Africans, and the Making of the Modern World, 1471 to the Second World War*, New York: Liveright.
11. According to the World Bank, poverty in sub-Saharan Africa has not fallen fast enough to keep up with population growth. An estimated 433m people were living in extreme poverty in 2018, up from 284m in 1990. World Bank (2020), "Poverty and Shared Prosperity 2020: Reversals of Fortune", Washington, DC

Europe did not escape the consequences of the crime committed against the birthplace of humanity. The inflow of Rents from the Caribbean deepened the divide between the rent seekers and the people whom they displaced from the commons.

How do we compensate the losers for those losses? In one way or another, everyone in the world, today, is a loser. Including the genuine free riders, like Donald Trump. How do we cover the cost of repairing the damage?

The third model of property rights was elaborated in Book 1 of *#WeAreRent*.

> ► *The evolutionary blueprint*. Solutions flow from this
> model. As will be explained in Book 3, Rent transcends
> nation-state borders and elevates progress to ever-higher
> planes of existence by sharing One-World Rent.

This model, however, can only emerge out of moral foundations. This creates a difficulty for those who insist on compensation, at the expense of other claimants. Two current cases illustrate the nature of the claims to compensation arising from the history created by the culture of free riding.

> ► UN special rapporteurs want the British government
> to deliver "effective remedies and reparations" for the
> Kipsigis and Talai peoples in Kenya. They were displaced
> from their land to make way for white settlers who
> wanted to establish tea plantations.[12]

> ► Following defeats in court, the Canadian government
> offered C$40bn (US$31bn; £23.6bn) compensation
> to indigenous children. Previous governments had
> sent them to boarding schools where many were
> malnourished, beaten and sexually abused.

---

12. www.theguardian.com/global-development/2021/aug/03/un-criticises-uk-for-failure-to-redress-colonial-era-land-grab-in-kenya

Some ended up in unmarked graves.[13] Children forced to abandon native languages and convert to Christianity implicated Canada in the crime against humanity.

On behalf of those who continue to be damaged by the culture of cheating, we need answers to these questions.

► Why should taxpayers who rent their homes (they do not enjoy capital gains) contribute to the compensation of landowners?

► Why should damage caused by the culture of cheating continue unabated, because money is not available to compensate landowners?

The list of awkward questions is a long one. It includes this moral challenge: is compensation payable to the noble owners of inherited estates? Or, rather, do they owe compensation to the generations of people whose lives were damaged by the enclosure of the commons on which their estates are situated?

The assault on society, guided by the nobility, continues to this day. A report commissioned by the Archbishop of Canterbury found that, in 2021, "Around 8 million people in England live in overcrowded, unaffordable, or unsuitable homes. That is not right. Whole sections of our society, including people of all ages, are affected by the housing crisis, but those caught in poverty bear the brunt of this injustice". This made it harder to maintain "stable communities". The Church of England, the one established by Henry VIII, is part of the problem. It squats on vacant land "suitable for the delivery of 28,500 new homes across England". The archbishop's report admitted:

> There is something fundamentally questionable about a system where, simply by owning land and doing nothing with it, the value of

that land increases over time to produce an unearned windfall gain. Income earned by work done is fair and just…[T]here is a just reason for intervention to stop the process whereby land values inevitably increase over time.[14]

Despite the demand for affordable dwellings, over 648,000 empty dwellings blighted the English urban landscape in 2019.[15] Absent is the pricing pressure on owners to put those dwellings to use. Empty homes do not yield rents, but the capital gains keep accumulating for their absent owners.

Towards a New Age

If there is to be a return to the path of evolutionary growth, who better to take the lead than people who were co-opted into the culture of cheating through the purchase of their homes? They have the most to lose; and the most to gain, depending on the choice they make.

Initiating change will not be easy. To violate human evolution, the culture of cheating had to embed itself ever-deeper into the human psyche, to smother thoughts that might impede rent seeking. To sustain itself, it had to mould its victims into one of two types of personalities.

▶ People who, although they do not inherit landed estates, assume the postures of the aristocracy. They are schooled in institutions like Eton and Oxford. Boris Johnson fits this profile. He displays the essential characteristics of irresponsibility in public affairs, opportunism in private matters, charming in demeanour, fit to hold high offices of state and preserve the culture of rent seeking.

14. *Coming Home: Tackling the Housing Crisis Together* (2021), p.5, 83. https://www. archbishopofcanterbury.org/priorities/coming-home
15. Wendy Wilson *et al* (2020), Empty Housing (England), House of Commons Library, Briefing Paper No 3012. file:///D:/Downloads/SN03012.pdf

► People who, although they acquire land beneath their homes, are willing to diligently work to produce the net income on which the predator culture relies to sustain itself. Such a character was Kevin Reeves (see Box 7.3).

One part of the truth and reconciliation process, therefore, must include coming to terms with such terrible intervention in people's lives.

If justice is to be restored at the heart of society, palliative measures – the modest fiscal gestures at municipal level – are not enough. The social status of Rent must be restored. Only then can the public's pricing mechanism serve as a system of information that delivers rich rewards through a liberated economy.

Consider the additional wealth and welfare that would arise from the reorganisation of just one industry. Fossil fuels were under-charged by government, to maximise the Rents of private owners. This inflicted a deadweight loss on our world that is now running at an annual rate of $3 trillion. The losses include disease and premature deaths from air pollution.[16] Under the revised pricing system, that $3 trillion becomes wealth and welfare distributed among everyone willing to work for their living.

To achieve that new world, however, a new approach to politics is needed. Conventional political parties cannot lead the way back to the evolutionary growth that harmonises relationships between people and between nations. Politicians, because of the ideological constraints within which they operate, are afflicted with what we might call the Caesar Syndrome. Even if Nero did not fiddle while Rome burnt in 64 A.D, the Caesars who succeeded him did "fiddle" their civilisation. They facilitated the culture of free riding. Rome's resilience was dissipated. They capitulated to a militarily inferior force. Rome was sacked in 455 AD.

---

16. John Doer (2021), *Speed & Scale*, London: Penguin Business, p.266.

Box 7.3 **Co-opted by the culture**

Kevin Reeves was orphaned as a child, raised in a convent and he left school at the age of 12 in a "barely literate" state.* He entered the labour market soon after Britain emerged from the post-war era of rationing. By the time he died in 2019, at the age of 71, Kevin had amassed a fortune of £100m. The money came from land.

Kevin was not schooled into the role of rent seeker. He found work in the construction industry, and became an entrepreneur: a land developer. By building houses, he helped to fulfil the needs and dreams of working families.

Part of his fortune came as windfalls. As the economy grew, the price of land rose in 18-year boom/bust cycles. Kevin was in the property market for the long run, so he could ride out the downturns and capture the gains from the upturns. He rendered a service to consumers, but in doing so he was unwittingly complicit in the culture of cheating.

* www.dailymail.co.uk/news/article-10262059/Siblings-war-barely-literate-fathers-100M-estate.html

---

People must take control of their destinies. Authentic democracy would follow from the cathartic conversations that deepened awareness of the structural flaws in the socio-economic system. Equipped with the knowledge of how to improve the lives of everyone willing to work for their wellbeing, people could then democratically mandate the relevant reforms.

The conversations should include the merits of governance based on Whole-of-Life budgets. This would be the first opportunity for the people of the commons to give their consent to the fiscal tools of their choice. Agreement is required on the relationship between public services and payments into the public purse. The obligations of elected representatives must be specified. The new constitutional settlement must affirm personal responsibilities.

The conversations would culminate in the drafting of a Bill of Rights and Responsibilities, to replace the proclamations sanctioned by the United Nations, European governments and the UK, which accommodate the culture of cheating.

For the first time in modern history, people would control the political process. They achieve this by demonstrating that each individual, through the willingness to work for personal needs, and to generate a net income, is the locus of authentic power. Without that productivity, it is not possible to sustain the structure of authority that complex societies need.

The innovative elements for engaging in constructive conversations are available.[17] These can be adapted for local, regional, national and international conversations between people of goodwill who are willing to listen and learn, rather than just talking at others. In the past, individuals like Adam Smith and Thomas Paine knew what needed to be done; but they were lone voices. Today, people have the capacity to communicate with others world-wide, and the practical strategies for making the difference are tried and tested – if they want structural change.

One thing is for sure. There is nowhere to hide from the collapse on the other side of the 2026 precipice.

With vision, we *can* navigate the Social Galaxy into a viable future. Visions are utopian only in the absence of practical strategies for bridging the chasm between here and there. By revitalising the fabric of humanity with the flow of Rental energy, re-empowered people would rebuild their lives and their communities. There is no need to be crushed back into a Dark Age. Or worse.

---

17. https://ic-uk.org.uk/

2026 Countdown

Time up! The choice is between protecting capital gains on homes, and the future of the family as a coherent unit. The cost of a home competes with the costs of raising children.[18] *Ann Berrington, professor of demography and social statistics, reports that "those who do manage to buy a home might well postpone or even forego having children. So the families that people may have planned to have will be unfulfilled". The rental sector "remains un-family friendly, unregulated, and insecure".*

---

18. Valentina Tocchioni *et al* 2021), "The Changing Association Between Homeownership and the Transition to Parenthood", *Demography* (https: / /doi .org /10 .1215 /00703370 -9420322)

Between Good and Evil

The choice unites every person on Earth. The choice between good and evil.

In Chapter 1, I cautioned against apocalyptic language that, in past times, intentionally evoked fear. Back then, there were good reasons to use those words: alert people to threats unseen, or not understood.

The danger today is in plain sight. The traces surround us in abundance, fully understood, but wilfully disregarded. I will classify it as Evil; and its alternative, as Good.

Either we cooperate on a global level to face down the Evil; or we share the terrible consequences.

My account of the Good model comes with a puzzle. If it is so virtuous, why have democratic societies, with their universal suffrage, managed to resist its adoption? They claim to be "open" in debate, vigorous in science and ethical in championing human rights. So why have people failed to authorise it? One illustration of the general answer to the conundrum is the rent seeker's law Donald Trump enacted, the Tax Cuts and Jobs Act (2017). As my final attempt to embed a clear understanding of the nature of the Evil model, therefore, I will review the free riding scam which Trump welcomed with a "bear-hug embrace".[1]

I conclude with a brief account of how, by combining the authentic forms of democracy, morality and justice, we can facilitate the transition to the Good society.

Opportunity for whom?

The billionaires of Silicon Valley really believed that they could invest their money to help low-income people in deprived neighbourhoods across the United States.

I do not doubt their sincerity.

If they had read my first book, however (published in 1983), they would have understood why they would fail. Margaret Thatcher had promoted "enterprise zones", which she hyped as a way to increase jobs and elevate wages in deprived neighbourhoods. The fiscal incentives, however, were calculated to deliver no such outcomes. Instead, they raised the value of land in yet another ATCOR-affirming exercise. *Cut taxes and the zero elasticity effect leaps into action. The benefits of lower taxes are captured in the form of Rent.* The zones did not stimulate enterprise on the scale desired by the host populations. Instead, they encrusted yet another layer of rent seeking indulgence on the backs of the working population. Subsequent exercises in promoting growth in "left-behind" locations were equally disappointing (Box E.1).

It is safe to assume that internet mogul Sean Parker, who implanted the idea of "opportunity zones" in the US, had not read *The Power in the Land*. With an abundance of money to splash around, he convinced himself that he could help spatially disadvantaged families by persuading other billionaires to pump money into deprived neighbourhoods. In the event, author David Wessel described the 8,700 zones as an "archipelago of

1. David Wessel (2021), *Only the Rich can Play*, New York: Public Affairs, p.276.

Box E.1 **Enterprising for whom?**

In the last two decades of the 20th century, 50 enterprise zones were operating in the UK. The House of Commons Library reviewed 21st century attempts to stimulate growth in such locations.

The National Audit Office, in *Funding and structures for local economic growth* (2013), examined two such exercises. It found that the long-term aim of attracting investment and jobs was obstructed by "short term financial incentives" which "create uncertainty for businesses". The government aim (expressed in 2011) of 54,000 jobs was disappointed: between 6,000 and 18,000 new jobs were expected by 2015.

In 2014, the House of Commons Public Accounts Committee published *Promoting Economic Growth Locally*. This revealed that, by December 2013, just 4,649 jobs (and 2,965 construction jobs) had been created by Enterprise Zones in England, which it described as "particularly underwhelming", when compared to the Treasury projections of 54,000 jobs.*

* House of Commons Library (2020), Enterprise Zones, Briefing Paper No 5942, p.10.

---

tax havens across the country". Parker admitted: "We couldn't anticipate where all of the holes would be". The outcomes ought not to have been a mystery: they were predictable. As one investor noted, land prices in the zones were "overpriced, driven up by the potential [zone] tax benefits, in inferior locations".

Rust Belt residents fell for the free riding scams because they came with the imprimatur of Trump, the man who personified Evil. At the same time, desperately impoverished people were induced to place their hope in False Flag exercises. Mayors in 32 cities, who pinned their faith in an exercise known as Universal Basic Income (UBI), flew one of those flags. They handed out, with no strings attached, money that was supposed to alleviate poverty. UBI is an example of how dreams of reformers are infected by palliative strategies. This approach to systemic crises, however, is the modern version of the Roman bread-and-circuses ploy: contain plebeian discontent to prolong the High Life of the elites in the dying decades of the empire.[2]

There is no shortage of examples of the effective remedy to poverty. Take the case of the British film industry, which received cuts in taxes to foster its activity. For every £1 of tax relief, the industry returned an additional £8.30 to the British economy in 2019.[3] That is one measure of the deadweight burden of conventional taxes. Donald Trump was the last person to tell his fans that this alternative – Good – model, was waiting in the wings.

The Good Model

Pooling Rent simultaneously addresses the multiple challenges we face in the moral, social, biological and material realms. They are all rooted in the perverse tax regime.

Scholars, schooled into confining research to veneer issues, do not explore this comprehensive solution. In relation to the ecological crisis, for example, the working assumption is that the dangerous trends in global temperatures originated with reckless economic growth, or because of globalisation, or the malign nature of technology. Their palliatives consequently accommodate the underlying – the organising – mechanism. The "targeted policies" are futile. They cannot erase problems that are symptoms of systemic failure. In relation to the Great Convergence of the four existential threats, nothing less than the Whole-of-Life approach will work.

---

2. The mayors were aware that poverty "is not a moral failing but a systemic one", but they lack the power to reshape the system. Patti Waldmeir (2021), "New basic income schemes divide the Midwest", *Financial Times*, Dec. 13.
3. British Film Industry (2021), Screen Business: How screen sector tax reliefs power economic growth across the UK 2017-2019, p.24. bfi.org.uk/screen-business

The correct diagnosis would redirect attention to ways of shifting behaviour across the whole spectrum of relationships. The one policy that achieves this rests on the obligation to pay the full Rent into the public purse for the benefits received from nature and society. This is Adam Smith's "invisible hand" at work, guiding behaviour that conforms to standards set by the partnership between ethics and efficiency. In the economic sphere, the pricing system organically unites the private marketplace with the public domain. This is achieved when people conform to the rule: "keep what you create, pay for what you receive". This rule adjusts behaviour in relation to consumer goods and public goods.

The UK already has the legislation on paper. Parliament can dust off the 1931 Budget and reshape some of the Land Tax clauses to take account of the Rent-creating opportunities of the Digital Age. The effects would be electrifying.

► *Socially:* communities rebuilt as children remained and repaired the infrastructure.

► *Psychologically:* mental health healed as hope replaced poverty and despair.

► *Economically:* sustainable growth as productivity increased from the bottom up.

People's trust in governance would recover as the buoyant budget funded the services they needed: more teachers and nurses, roads repaired, traumas of the past replaced by a vitality based on the freedom to work and realise personal aspirations. People would monitor for themselves the rehabilitation of communities across the whole spectrum of activities, including recreational and artistic pursuits (features of Culture in Fig. E.1).

International trade, resource extraction from nature, rebuilding the Social Galaxy, they would all automatically benefit from the authentic freedom that merged the imperatives of ethics and efficiency.

Figure E.1 **the Rent-revenue synergy**

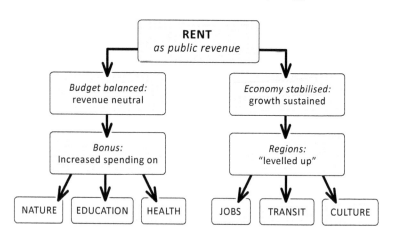

The transition

Plotting the transition out of the Covid pandemic is the perfect prelude to planning for the converging crises post-2026. The most effective way to memorialise the people who lost their lives to the virus from nature would be to exorcise, in their names, the perverse virus from society.

The phased transition should take place over 10 years (two electoral terms), with taxation redesigned on a revenue-neutral basis: every £1 tax cut offset by £1 raised from Rent.

The first cuts should favour those sectors that are least vulnerable to the ATCOR effect. In the case of the UK film industry, the benefits from the tax cuts gravitated to employees and investors who produced the movies, not to the owners of Rent-generating assets. Agriculture, however, is a classic case in which changes to the tax regime immediately surface in the land market.

Subsidies to farmers are shifted at speed to the owners of farmland. Tax cuts drive up the rent of farmland. Fiscal reforms to the farm sector, therefore, must be carefully introduced to protect food production and the welfare of the workforce.

Planning should be guided by the need to

▶ *Create jobs and raise wages: the short term*

▶ *Contain debt and balance the books: the medium term*

▶ *Cultivate restructuring: the long-term*

Transformation requires the informed consent of the population. Everyone must have the opportunity to engage in conversations about priorities.

▶ If unemployment is at the top of the agenda, cut the Income Tax. If capital formation is a critical need, cut the corporation tax and subsidies that distort capital markets.

▶ If housing affordability is the priority, accelerate location charges to offset the construction industry's decline (-35%) that resulted from the pandemic.[4]

▶ If cleaning up the banking sector is essential, reforms must avoid a financial meltdown of the kind that occurred in 2008.

By developing a nuanced transition programme, people ("the market") would smoothly adjust behaviour without the need for diktats from governments. The Rent strategy achieves personal and societal goals with the minimum of administrative effort for the maximum returns. Synergy is one version of the "wisdom of the crowd". This prospectus contrasts with what happened in the three last attempts at "building back better" in the UK.

---

4. The market would not wait for Parliament, if investors were convinced that change was coming. Vacant land, which is hoarded, would be quickly brought into use.

► First, after WW2: Labour governments' socialist reforms ended in chaos with worker strikes in the early 1970s, which included the Winter of Discontent.

► Second: Margaret Thatcher's Big Bang financial reforms shifted corporate strategies from capital formation to the "bonus" culture and the dot.com bubble.

► Third, the "too big to fail" syndrome of 2008 resulted in austerity and the regulatory regime, which were abruptly terminated by the pandemic.

Box E.2 **Authentic independence**

The people of Scotland would ask, "Why is Scotland the No.1 European country for deaths by drugs?" The deaths are not, in the main, the idiosyncratic failures of weak personalities; they are part of the chain reaction to the dysfunctional social structure.

As a matter of policy, the government in Edinburgh decided not to modify the tax regime. Under powers devolved from Westminster in 2016, it had the right to redesign the Income Tax. It could zero rate the tax in a revenue-neutral strategy, replacing the income with a property tax based on location values. The SNP government declined to do so, despite repeated representations from the Scottish Land Revenue Group.*

Instead, the SNP raised rates of income taxation. The outcome was predictable, as documented in the Scottish Fiscal Commission's *Economic and Fiscal Forecasts* (Dec. 2021). Scotland is sliding deeper into the fiscal vortex: slower growth of the economy than the rest of the UK, and slower growth in tax revenue. This, coupled with an increase in welfare spending, delivers the gift of an ever-increasing fiscal burden to future generations.

If the people of Scotland want to heal the scars bequeathed by the clearances of the clans, they can do so by authorising the tax reform that would deliver a healthy, wealthy, and inclusive society. That is authentic independence.

*https://slrg.scot/

Citizens' Assemblies would enable people to converse in regional communities and on the national scale, leading to the informed mandate for changes to governance. The Assemblies, for example, could commission research into the medical condition of the population, to reveal the roots that result in unequal life expectancy; and to understand discrimination against people in "peripheral" regions (Box E.2).

The revenue-neutral transition would abolish deadweight taxes, with some "sin" taxes retained if the intentional intervention in behaviour was appropriate. Life chances would be equalised across the economic catchment area in an authentic "levelling up" process. The full elaboration of this strategy is the subject of Book 3.

Epilogue

In December 2021, the Johnson Government proposed a new Bill of Rights "to restore a proper balance between the rights of individuals, personal responsibility and the wider public interest". The Bill must include the responsibilities of Parliament and the democratic process. Institutions and policies that implicate the people of Britain in the crime against humanity must be eliminated. The government promises to undertake "a full Impact Assessment" of its proposals. Book 3 of #WeAreRent holds the UK government, and its Impact Assessment, to account.

The ATCOR seesaw

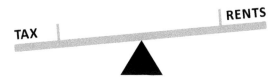

Adam Smith understood the seminal nature of Rent. A nation's net income is located at the interface between people's private lives and their social institutions.

Rent serves as the fulcrum point in the system that balances earned and unearned incomes. It is the ultimate determinant of the wealth of the nation. No matter how hard people may work, they need the services funded out of Rent to complement their labours, if they are to avoid destitution.

The gravitational pull-and-push between wages, profits and Rent emerges in the marketplace as negotiations between consumers and producers. The deals, sealed through the pricing mechanism, take place at the interface with governance. The outcome – the distribution of income – works in seesaw fashion. So, when (in the UK) Pitt the Younger's government introduced the Income Tax in 1799, the pressure shifted in favour of an increase in household incomes. The increase would compensate for the loss of revenue through taxation. That increase could come from one source only: the Rent that flowed to those who owned land. Conversely, if, today, government abolished the Income Tax, the seesaw pressure would shift in favour of an increase in Rent. That response would be most immediately visible in the residential property market, in the form of higher prices paid for land.

The impact of the seesaw effects depends on the way income is distributed. The single most important issue is the status of Rent. In its social form, there are no losers. Everyone would benefit, through equal access to the services funded out of the public purse. Under the current tax-and-tenure regime, however, the beggar-thy-neighbour attitudes of the culture of free riding would distort the outcomes. Rather than receive a lower Rent, for example, landowners can, and do, withhold land from people who wish to use it. Because of the power they exercise, they can arbitrarily tilt markets in their favour.

Smith explained how the indirect collection of Rent, in the form of taxes on wages and profits, imposed enormous losses on the wealth of the nation. Taxes distorted people's behaviour. To avoid the *indirect* collection of Rent, they ducked and weaved in a thousand-and-one ways, the net effect of which was to reduce economic productivity. *The Wealth of Nations*, therefore, was not just a text on economics; it was a manual on the science of good governance. The economic distortions faded away when governments collected revenue directly from Rent. That was why he recommended that the state should collect its revenue in the form of a Ground Rent

Today, people are intuitively aware that there is a fundamental problem with their public finances. Politically, however, the alternative is taboo. Even when economists feel obliged to note the virtues of the direct collection of Rent to fund public services, they are careful to provide politicians with the excuse not to reflect further on the policy implications. They do this by claiming that the quantum of Rent is insufficient to eliminate the taxes that constrain people from achieving their aspirations. Erik Brynjolfsson, a professor at the MIT Sloan School of Management, and his colleague Andrew McAfee, assert:

> The 19th century economist Henry George took this insight and argued that we should have just a single tax, a land tax. While an enticing idea, the reality is that revenues from land rents aren't high enough to pay for all government services.[1]

The Experts work with shallow analytical models that fail to "follow the money" to its final destination. A tax liability may be split (for example) between an employee and employer, but these trigger further ripple effects. One of the ripples emerges as the seesaw effect: a rise in the tax burden reduces the sum that remains as Rent in the marketplace. The reduced Rent is capitalised into a lower selling price of land. When, *vice versa*, there is a cut in the tax burden, people retain more disposable income. Landowners step in to capture that gain by increasing the commercial rents of dwellings, or increasing the sale price of land.

Once upon a time, lawmakers understood this dynamic process. A century ago, when a Liberal government sought to apply a direct levy on Rent in the UK, Winston Churchill explained the economic implications (Box A.1).

By taking into account the incidence of taxes – that is, their ultimate destination – we achieve a robust breakdown of a nation's annual income. In the richer OECD countries, Rent is about 50% of national income. About 30% of national income is *indirectly* collected from Rent in the form of taxes on "income" or "profits" or levies on goods and services. The rest, about 20% as measurable in the marketplace, is Rent in its privatised form.

The ATCOR thesis – all taxes come out of Rent – can be traced back to John Locke. He reported that taxes on wages reduced take-home pay below what people needed

---

1. E. Brynjolfsson and A. McAfee (2014), *The Second Machine Age*, New York: W.W. Norton, p.227.

Box A.1 **Churchill & the toll bridge**

Winston Churchill illustrated ATCOR with the economics of a toll bridge across the Thames. People crossed the bridge to work in the City of London. A daily toll of one penny was levied. When the owners were bought out with public money, commuters could cross the bridge and save sixpence a week. Within a very short time rents on the south side of the river were raised by about sixpence a week!

In another example, recounted in a Commons speech in 1909, Churchill noted how "in the parish of Southwark, about £350 a year was given away in doles of bread by charitable people in connection with one of the churches. As a consequence of this the competition for small houses, but more particularly for single-room tenements, is, we are told, so great that rents are considerably higher than in the neighbouring district.

"All goes back to the land, and the land owner...is enabled with resistless strength to absorb to himself a share of almost every public and every private benefit, however important or however pitiful those benefits may be."*

*www.wealthandwant.com/docs/Churchill_TPL.html

---

to live on. This caused workers to defend their living standards by reducing the Rent that they paid for the use of land. *Ergo*: ATCOR in action. What governments collect in revenue is – ultimately – at the expense of Rent. Locke's insight was published in *Some Considerations on the Consequences of the Lowering of Interest and the Raising of the Value of Money* (1691). In the 19th century, ATCOR was even the subject of literary treatment by people like George Bernard Shaw (Box A.2).

The conclusion is of profound significance. *By one route or another, people are already paying for public services out of Rent.* This means that Rent is more than sufficient to fund existing public services. The roundabout route, however, imposes a terrible price in the form of

---

Box A.2 **The 3-card trick**

Lower production costs, and government spending, automatically mutate into higher Rents. George Bernard Shaw offered a literary exposition of this process. His illustration will resonate today with people who are quitting dense urban centres for more spacious rural or suburban locations.

Shaw stressed that the exodus from inner cities did not leave families financially better off. Why? Commuting costs offset the lower suburban rents. There is no net gain from the relocation. Rent captures the net income, *after people have covered their tax liabilities and the other costs of living*. Landowners "can strip them of everything except what is barely enough to keep them alive to earn money for the landowner, and bring up families to do the same in the next generation".*

Today, ATCOR has been "disappeared" from economic texts, victim of the street magician's 3-card trick: *now you see it, now you don't*.

* G.B.Shaw (1928), *The Intelligent Woman's Guide to Socialism and Capitalism*, London: Constable, p.125.

---

losses at all levels of being – biological, psychological and sociological. Post-classical economists respond to those distortions by urging governments to cut taxes. They do not advertise the complementary reform: funding public services out of Rent. There are exceptions. Nobel Prize winner Joseph Stiglitz is one of them. He recognises that, to rebuild communities after the pandemic, solutions must address the "poorer-performing economy marked by greater rent seeking and greater inequality".[2] That can only happen by applying the principles of good governance.

---

2. Joseph Stiglitz (2020), "Conquering the Great Divide", *Finance & Development*, Sept., p.18.

Good governance

The ATCOR thesis was at the core of Adam Smith's account of the science of good governance, the cornerstone of his model of an ethics-based economy. A revenue system that harmonised prices in the private markets with payments into the public purse would free people to go about their business without consciously taking into account what was happening in the rest of society. By pooling the annual Ground Rent, people would automatically fulfil their social responsibilities. Smith's aphorism for this was "the invisible hand" in action.

If lawmakers *had* adopted Smith's model of govern-ance, they would have removed the taxes on wages and savings. Those taxes, Smith stressed, were futile, if the goal was to enhance economic activity. He provided at least 10 examples of how Rent, in one form or another, was the basis of government revenue. Direct collection was the correct strategy, because "no discouragement will thereby be given to any sort of industry. The annual produce of the land and labour of the society, the real wealth and revenue of the great body of the people, might be the same after such a tax as before". [3]

Ground Rents, therefore, were "the species of revenue which can best bear to have a peculiar tax imposed upon them". This contrasted with a tax on a manufacturer, who passed the burden on as higher prices paid by consumers. Consumers, in turn, would be left with less income, which meant they had to reduce the Rent paid to landlords. A tax levied on the producer would ultimately result in "a reduction of rent, the final payment of the tax would fall upon the landlord".

Auditing the taxable capacity of a nation entailed no difficulty if the revenue came from Rent.[4] Rent neutralised the temptation

---

3. Page references are to the 1976 edition of *The Wealth of Nations*, edited by Edwin Cannan and published by the University of Chicago Press.
4. Bk 5, Ch 2, Pt 2, Article 1, pp. 370, 374-375.

to dodge taxes by transferring assets to tax havens. Why? Because "the quantity and value of the land which any man possesses can never be a secret, and can always be ascertained with great exactness". This contrasted with taxing goods, which caused "endless vexation as no people could support". Smith noted the obvious: "land is a subject which cannot be removed, whereas stock easily may".

Ground Rent and houses

For Smith, "Ground-rents are a still more proper subject of taxation than the rent of houses". The reason for his advocacy was simple: a charge levied directly on location Rent would not raise the rents that people paid for their dwellings. That levy would fall on the owner of the Ground Rent, who was already exacting "the greatest rent which can be got for the use of his ground". If the tax were levied on the tenant, "the less he would incline to pay for the ground; so that the final payment of the tax would fall altogether upon the owner of the ground-rent". Raising revenue from Ground Rent was reasonable, because the owner received Rent "without any care or attention of his own".[5]

House prices and the Window Tax

Smith objected to the taxation of windows. He emphasised that "The natural tendency of the window-tax, and of all other taxes upon houses, is to lower rents. The more a man pays for the tax, the less, it is evident, he can afford to pay for the rent". Increases in the rent of dwellings, however, had more than offset the taxes on windows. This was because of the rising demand for dwellings; it did not falsify the theory. As Smith drily noted: "Had it not been for the tax, rents would probably have risen still higher".[6]

---

5. Bk 5, Ch 2, Pt 2, Article 1, p.370.
6. Bk 5, Ch 2, Pt 2, Article 1, p.373.

Taxes on the profits of farming

A tenant farmer would not reduce his output in response to a tax levied directly on his profit. Instead, Smith observed, to protect his profit, the farmer would end up "paying less rent to the landlord. The more he is obliged to pay in the way of tax, the less he can afford to pay in the way of rent". [7]

The Poll Tax on slaves

Smith tracked the impact of the Poll Tax levied on slaves in the English colonies in the Carolinas of America and the islands of the West Indies. Those taxes, Smith explained, reduced the profits of the agricultural enterprises. So: "As the planters are, the greater part of them, both farmers and landlords, the final payment of the tax falls upon them in their quality of landlords without any retribution". [8]

Taxes on the sale of property

Taxes levied on property at the point of sale place bargaining power in the hands of the buyer. "He considers what the land will cost him in tax and price together," observed Smith. "The more he is obliged to pay in the way of tax, the less he will be disposed to give in the way of price." So the tax on land is passed on in the form of a lower price paid to the vendor of land. [9]

A tax on the wages of labour

Smith carefully analysed the chaos caused by a tax on wages. Whichever way the burden is twisted (reducing profits, raising the price of consumer goods or inflating the wages paid to workers), there is no escaping the ultimate outcome:

---

7. Bk 5, Ch 2, Pt 2, Article 2, p.383.
8. Bk 5, Ch 2, Pt 2, Article 2, p.384.
9. Bk 5, Ch 2, Pt 2, Arts. 1 & 2, p.390.

> In all cases a direct tax upon the wages of labour must, in the long-run, occasion both a greater reduction in the rent of land, and a greater rise in the price of manufactured goods, than would have followed upon the proper assessment of a sum equal to the produce of the tax, partly upon the rent of land, and partly upon consumable commodities.

Smith branded those taxes as "absurd and destructive". He was emphatic about their disruptive effects.

> The declension of industry, the decrease of employment for the poor, the diminution of the annual produce of the land and labour of the country, have generally been the effects of such taxes. In consequence of them, however, the price of labour must always be higher than it otherwise would have been in the actual state of the demand: and this enhancement of price, together with the profit of those who advance it, must always be finally paid by the landlords and consumers.

The consumers to whom Smith referred were the rich landowners who enjoyed "conspicuous consumption".

One detects sorrow in Smith's words as he recorded how, while the deadweight burden of bad taxes did, ultimately, come out of Rent, the circuitous route victimised the poor by pricing them out of work.[10]

Taxes on the "necessaries of life"

In the 18th century, the principal taxes on the "necessaries of life" fell on salt, leather, soap and candles. Those taxes triggered increases in wages, but the charges would ultimately "fall upon the rent of the landlord". Again, Smith expresses the bitter consequences, which included the "forced frugality" imposed on working people. Other outcomes included a reduction in fertility, and the resort to immoral behaviour. Immorality affected children whose parents were impoverished. If the children survived the hardships to which the bad conduct of their parents exposed them, such conduct commonly corrupted their morals, "so that, instead of being useful to society

---

10. Bk 5, Ch 2, Pt 2, Art. 3, p.392-4.

by their industry, they become public nuisances by their vices and disorders". Bad fiscal policy equated with human suffering.

> Taxes upon necessaries, so far as they affect the labouring poor, are finally paid, partly by landlords in the diminished rent of their lands, and partly by rich consumers, whether landlords or others in the advanced price of manufactured goods; and always with a considerable over charge.

Landlords "always pay in a double capacity; in that of landlords, by the reduction of their rent; and in that of rich consumers, by the increase of their expense".[11]

The tax on wine

Smith arrived at the same conclusion when he analysed the economics of a tax on the production of wine. "The whole weight of the tax, therefore, would fall upon the rent and profit; properly upon the rent of the vineyard." Producers of commodities such as sugar were aware of this effect, so they asserted that a tax on output would not fall on consumers, but would reduce the Rent they received as plantation owners. Smith pointed out that this argument demonstrated that the tax levied on the Rent of plantation land was an appropriate charge.[12]

The impact of tithes

Traditionally, communities supported their church and clergy by allocating a proportion of their net produce as a tithe. Again, that charge "diminishes more what would otherwise be the rent of the landlord". Smith reviewed the relative virtues of a Land Tax compared to a tithe in the colonies compared to the charge levied on rent-rolls in Great Britain. He saw no reason to alter his conclusion: one way or another, the charge came out of Rent. "There is no farmer who does not compute beforehand what the church tithe, which is

---

11. Bk 5, Ch 2, Pt 2, Art. 4, p.400-403.
12. Bk 5, Ch 2, Pt 2, Art. 4, p.424-425.

a land-tax in kind, is, one year with another, likely to amount to."[13] The farmer made "a proportionable abatement in the rent which he agrees to pay to the landlord".[14]

Adam Smith provided the manual of the science of good governance.

Today, macro-economists omit from their calculations the enormous losses arising from the circuitous collection of Rent via taxes. The omission is intentional: silence means they do not have to explain why people endure the deadweight losses. The debate on Rent, and taxation, is ring-fenced.

For their part, the earliest land-grabbers accepted the loss to the nation as the price for consolidating their privileges. Cossetted in their rural retreats, behind the walls of their mansions, they did not suffer the consequences.

The fiscal failure of governance, Adam Smith stressed, results in mass distress, the loss of economic productivity and the indebtedness of governments.[15] That indebtedness, as measured across the global economy, reached nearly $300tn in the second quarter of 2021.[16]

---

13. Bk 5, Ch 2, Pt 2, Art. 1, p.362
14. Bk 5, Ch 3, p.472.
15. Bk 5, Ch 3, p.464-465.
16. Estimate by the Institute of International Finance. www.iif.com/Research/Capital-Flows-and-Debt/Global-Debt-Monitor

Edward Luce, the *Financial Times*' editor in the United States, alluded to the existential implications when he drew attention to "Rome-style inequality" in America.[17] Under the cloak of ignorance, the culture of cheating cannibalised the vitality of classical Rome. The city's Caesars did not have access to Adam Smith's manual of good governance.

We do.

But will we read it?

17. Edward Luce (2021), "Democrats show little inclination to confront inequality head-on", *Financial Times*, Sept. 17.

About the author

Fred Harrison is an economic forecaster and policy analyst. Ten years before the financial crisis of 2008, he alerted governments that house prices would peak in 2007, which would trigger a banking crisis and economic depression. They failed to take defensive action. Applying the same methodology, the author has assessed the impact of Covid-19 and he predicts that house prices will peak in 2026. Our world is on course for a global catastrophe, unless nations mobilise the democratic consent that is needed to adopt the financial reforms that would mitigate the looming disasters.

Harrison is a graduate of the Universities of Oxford and London. After a career in Fleet Street journalism, he turned to the study of public policy and the way in which the global community of nations had been captured by the culture that reshaped western civilisation. His *Power in the Land* (1983) (2nd edn. 2021) set the scene for investigations leading to *The Traumatised Society* (2012). Most of his books are available at

https://shepheard-walwyn.co.uk/

To follow his campaign for a democratic reform of governance,

follow #WeAreRent

and visit www.wearerent.com

For more information on Rent, read Fred Harrison's analyses at

www.sharetherents.org

Acknowledgements

I had to travel extensively around the world to gather the materials that inform this volume. Many people kindly assisted me in that sojourn. Those who responded to requests for information for the present study include Nicolaus Tideman, Mary Cleveland, Fred Foldvary, Roger Sandilands, Dirk Löhr, Ed Dodson, Cliff Cobb, Bryan Kavanagh, Peter Meakin, Per Möller Anderson, Peter Challen and last, but not least, Heather Remoff.

I am indebted to Ian Kirkwood for his preparation of the graphics that illustrate this volume.

Valuable assistance was derived from
Land Research Trust **www.landresearchtrust.org**
The Scottish Land Revenue Group **www.slrg.scot**

Key concepts that frame the thesis of this book appear separately in the Rent Index (page 188).

Index

Rent Index

Also by Fred Harrison…

#We Are Rent

Book 1

Capitalism, Cannibalism
and why we must outlaw
Free Riding

Every nation on Earth today is at the mercy of what economists call free riding. Laws on taxation and land tenure were enacted to enable the aristocracy to get rich by riding on the backs of people who work for their living. It will not be possible to "build back better" after the Covid pandemic if governments continue to refuse to reform the way they tax earned incomes. A new narrative is needed which empowers people to take control of their destinies. Book 1 explains how early humans, through trial and error, established what became humanity's evolutionary blueprint. That blueprint is the tool for rethinking the destiny of human beings.

Forthcoming by Fred Harrison…

We Are Rent

Book 3

One-world Rent
and the Social Galaxy

The global community of nations is on course for upheavals that cannot be avoided by resurrecting the policies that have repeatedly failed in the past. One strategy alone would provide the synergy to mobilise nation-states behind the common cause of humanity. Fred Harrison explains the political significance of cross-border sharing of a stream of value which all nations help to create. One-world Rent is the blueprint that would initiate, for the first time on planet Earth, an age of inclusive peace and prosperity. Communities would be empowered to expand personal freedom while initiating new approaches to global trade and the renewal of the environment. The outcome would be a reinvigorated Social Galaxy.